100 Things To See In The Kimberley

By local guide Scotty Connell

SECOND EDITION

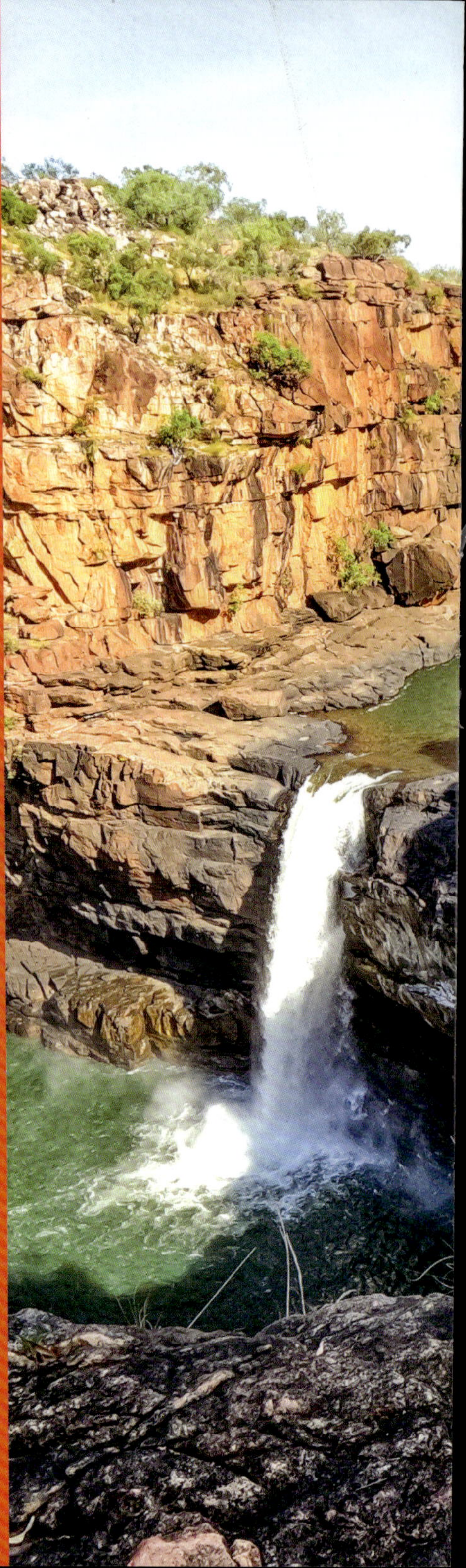

Exploring Eden Media

FOREWORD

When I first ventured into the Kimberley, I was blown away to find out the region is the size of Germany. I embarrassingly realised I had always thought it was kind of like the national park sizes I was used to, growing up in Victoria and NSW. You know, big, but not big enough that you could hide a fairly large country in it.

It really is a lot of space, and the sheer vastness (well, "bigness" was the word that came to mind, but I decided to use something more poetic) is something my tiny city-adapted mind struggled to comprehend when flying over it, let alone exploring it on foot. But as the vastness seeps into you, it brings with it a sense of magic in the Kimberley. The feeling that anything could be out there, maybe unseen and untouched by humans for thousands of years, or maybe, ever. No matter where you're standing, you can't shake the feeling that you and your lifespan is laughably tiny in this place.

The Kimberley is ever-changing, the landscape feels alive. You don't feel like you have visited a static place that's the same day in, day out; you feel like you visited a place that was a certain way, on a certain day, never to be quite the same again. That was the lasting feeling for me: I went away feeling like I shared a special moment with the land. I'm not sure how the land felt; I hope it remembers me, but having said that, I understand it meets a lot of people, and it must be tough to remember all of us.

To meaningfully connect and explore in a place of German-sized proportions, you have two options. Wander around aimlessly for years and years, hoping you discover the magical pockets and treasures the Kimberley has waiting for you (seems inefficient), or use the knowledge of someone who has lived and breathed the place and knows the land and its secrets by heart. I would definitely recommend the latter strategy, and the man to share that knowledge is Scotty. His knowledge of the place, what makes its nooks and crannies special, and indeed where they are, is something he's literally spent a life honing. I loved how he saw things in the land, and the wry smile he'd get as he'd tell you about a spot somewhere over a nearby mountain range or up a nearby waterway. This book is a shortcut to the things that give him those smiles. I know you'll use it to have your own special moment with the land in the Kimberley.

Hamish

CONTENTS

INTRODUCTION

There are two main reasons why the Kimberley is such a special place, and these two things constitute what I like to call the 'Kimberley spirit'.

First of all, there's the spirit of the people: those who were raised on this land and whose families have lived here for generations (like my wife, Taminga), and those who have wandered here, had life-enriching experiences and chosen to call it home.

Secondly, there's the spirit of the land: the vast areas of untamed wilderness, the incredible contrast between harsh landscapes and breathtaking scenery, and the total immersion in nature. There's a constant element of discovery, whether you have just arrived or have lived here for a lifetime.

As a tour guide, my mission is to showcase the Kimberley spirit to anyone who is open to receiving it. There's a local saying that up here, "A day can feel like a week, and a week can change the way you feel forever". I completely agree with this. I believe that if you come to the Kimberley with an open heart and mind, you will leave feeling richer in ways you'd never dream of.

As a young fella in Broome, I'd listen with great intrigue as my neighbour, Malcolm Douglas, would regale stories about his wild adventures into the far reaches of the Kimberley. My adolescence was dedicated to exploring the Kimberley. By air, land and sea, I have been a skipper and tour guide. I have also been a guest speaker representing Tourism Australia and Western Australia, both domestically and abroad. In my off-seasons, I've worked in Indigenous communities and embarked on foot expeditions to learn as much about the country as possible. I then set up Kimberley Spirit Tours, which has seen me both blessed and tested over the years while navigating this extraordinary yet unforgiving wilderness.

I've witnessed Purnululu National Park in full, wet season flood. I've mourned the passing of an old friend at El Questro, only to be greeted by a double rainbow as I left his memorial. I've administered first aid to my greatest mentor and friend after he was struck by a king brown snake at a remote coastal camp. I've found a saltwater crocodile lying under my brother's car (yep, you read that correctly). I've encountered thousands of Indigenous rock art sites and unnamed waterfalls. Over the years, some of the greatest people I've ever met – young and old – have become good friends while sharing the Kimberley spirit.

The Kimberley spirit isn't just about receiving; there's plenty that visitors can do to give back, from keeping areas pristine by picking up rubbish, to purchasing souvenirs and art directly from local people and Indigenous communities. In 2014 I founded the Kimberley Spirit Foundation, and we have a weekly food outreach where we deliver food and engage with young people in our community. I often feel 'fuelled up' after these food deliveries, even though it can be challenging and physically exhausting to put it all together.

The Kimberley is unlike other parts of Australia, and at times it feels like we're in a time warp, twenty years behind the rest of the nation. Here, we don't live by conventional time, but by tides, seasons and sunshine hours. Many places listed in this book will change completely from season to season: waterfalls will evaporate each Dry Season, and Wet Season floods will rearrange landscapes. Then there are the huge tides that make attractions appear and disappear daily. This is all part of the Kimberley's mystery.

I travel this country with the utmost respect and admiration for its traditional custodians, who have lived in harmony with this land for thousands of years.

The Kimberley is one of the world's great remaining wilderness areas, and, like many 'Kimberley kids', I feel privileged to live and work here. I hope that you embrace the Kimberley with a child-like sense of wonder, the same way that I felt when I was a boy listening to Malcolm's stories. May the Kimberley spirit enrich you and perhaps also inspire you to help us protect the region for the next generation.

From the desert to the sea, I love the Kimberley. I hope you do, too, and I hope you feel the spirit.

Scotty

Owner, Kimberley Spirit Tours
kimberleyspirit.com

TRAVEL IN THE KIMBERLEY

The Kimberley is one of Australia's last largely untouched wilderness areas. It's almost twice the size of Victoria but with only a twentieth of Victoria's roads and around six million fewer people. This is a land of extreme beauty, extreme weather and extreme wonder. Travelling here is an adventure, however you do it.

THE WEATHER

Located north of the Tropic of Capricorn, the Kimberley has a tropical monsoon climate. There's no summer or winter here, just Wet or Dry!

The Dry Season (May-Aug)

The days are cooler, and the skies are blue. Coastal areas experience cool, breezy nights while inland temperatures can plummet close to freezing.

The Build-Up (Sept-Nov)

In the lead-up to the Wet Season, temperatures and humidity increase, and waterholes dry up or stagnate. This is a good time for barramundi fishing. Plan your adventures for early morning or late afternoon. Avoid venturing out in the midday sun.

The Wet Season (Dec-Apr)

The Kimberley typically receives 90% of its rainfall during this season. National parks and roads close, and cyclones form offshore. Photographically, this is becoming an increasingly popular time to visit to capture epic lightning shows and waterfalls. Days are typically humid and muggy. As the 'run off' begins, it's also the best time to catch a barra.

GETTING TO THE KIMBERLEY

By road

There's an annual pilgrimage of 4WDs, campers, grey nomads and backpacker vans to the Kimberley each year. From the south, it's bitumen all the way along the Great Northern Highway, but to add some perspective, it's at least a 2,000km (1,250 mile) drive from WA's capital of Perth. And longer if you stick to the coast and check out a few things from the companion guide, 100 Things To See On Australia's Coral Coast.

If you're visiting from the Northern Territory, it's bitumen most of the way from Katherine to Kununurra (520km, 323 miles) along the Victoria Highway, with fuel available at Victoria River and Timber Creek. Another more adventurous route is via the Tanami Road from Alice Springs to Halls Creek (1,050km, 652 miles). That's nearly all dirt, and you'll need a 4WD vehicle to help deal with the corrugations. It also helps if you can drive over 500km (300 miles) between fuel stops (which occasionally run out of fuel). It's not a

difficult road, but it is remote, so come prepared.

Within the Kimberley, 4WDs are the go but are not required to tackle significant parts of the countryside. From Broome, you can travel up the Dampier Peninsula, out to Derby, to Kununurra and to Wyndham on bitumen. But a 4WD does give you access to the 660km-long, unsealed Gibb River Road and plenty of great side tracks, beaches, campsites and remote areas.

By air

During the peak winter months, QANTAS, Virgin and Airnorth operate regular flights to Broome and Kununurra.

Broome has daily direct flights from Perth, and on certain days of the week, there are direct flights from Darwin, Sydney, Melbourne and Brisbane.

Kununurra has daily direct flights from Darwin and direct flights from Perth on certain days of the week.

Several of the remote, exclusive resorts have their own airstrips. For some, this is the only access as there are no roads. You can charter private flights from Broome, Kununurra and Darwin if you're fortunate enough to visit these resorts.

Qantas
qantas.com.au
Phone 13 13 13

Virgin Australia
virginaustralia.com
Phone 13 67 89

Airnorth
airnorth.com.au
Phone 1800 627 474

LOCAL TIP:
Pack essentials (undies, swimwear, toiletries and a change of clothes) in case your luggage goes astray. The airport code for Broome, BME, is similar to Brisbane, BNE, which has caused luggage to end up in the wrong place many times before.

SALTWATER CROCODILES

"I'll tell you what, if there's one animal you wouldn't want to meet in a dark alley, it's a saltwater croc. Fortunately, they don't live in dark alleys, preferring saltwater instead"
– Russell Coight.

Don't be fooled by their name. Saltwater crocodiles, also known as estuarine crocodiles, inhabit rivers, lagoons, billabongs and waterholes across the Kimberley, thriving in fresh and saltwater and offshore islands. Unfortunately, there are often no warning signs in remote areas, so always check before jumping into any body of water. If in doubt, stay out. Avoid standing close to (or camping near) the water's edge. Just because you can't see them, it doesn't mean they're not there.

INSURANCE

When accidents happen in remote pockets of the Kimberley, medical evacuation by helicopter is a likely result. This can be extremely expensive. For this reason, I recommend purchasing travel insurance that covers remote area medi-evac (double check with your insurer. Some credit card insurances don't cover this).

Many parts of the Kimberley have higher than average crime rates, particularly regarding vehicle and property theft. Usually, things are safe within the grounds of the tourist-focussed businesses, but avoid leaving your car parked down a dark street at night with valuables visible. Check that your insurance covers valuables, including your camera.

TRAVELLING WITH DOGS

Travelling the Kimberley with your dog is entirely possible, and plenty of folks do. Many campsites and a handful of caravan parks allow dogs, but creating a dog friendly itinerary can be difficult if you're moving around. Dogs aren't allowed in any of the national parks (including Purnululu, Mitchell Falls, Windjana and Geikie Gorges and Wolfe Creek), and options are limited in Broome and Kununurra.

There are some particular dangers for dogs in the region, including saltwater crocodiles, 1080 baits, poisonous snakes, ticks and the stifling heat (especially inside the car). Always park in the shade and don't leave them inside the car. If you're tying them up, allow the lead to run under the car so that they can sit under there.

If your dog does need help, Broome Veterinary Clinic is the best bet in the west (owned by my mate Dave Morrell). It also has a boarding service. Phone (08) 9192 1319. In Kununurra, head to Kimberley Vet Centre phone (08) 9169 1229.

FUEL AND MECHANICS

We're a long way from the conveniences that are in the cities. Fuel comes into the ports of Wyndham and Broome and also by truck. It can be quite expensive, especially in the more remote areas along the Gibb River Road, where it can get to almost a dollar more at times. It always pays to have some extra budget put aside, in case they're higher than usual. One tip is to always get fuel where you can. Even if you don't need it at the time, fill up, as trucks and supplies experience unwanted delays regularly, and you can get caught out waiting in places you hadn't planned for by not having enough to get you to the next fuel spot.

Across the 660km Gibb River Road, you can usually get diesel and petrol at El Questro and Mt Barnett Roadhouse, and diesel (only) at Imintji Store. You'll have to carry enough fuel to get at least 350km between El Questro and Mt Barnett Roadhouse, not including any side trips. In Kalumburu and the Mitchell Plateau, you can get diesel and petrol. On the Dampier Peninsula, the Djarindjin Roadhouse is the only place to get fuel, 200km north of Broome. Things change, though, so call ahead or check in with the visitor centres before you leave.

You can get minor mechanical repairs at Mt. Barnett Roadhouse and Derby. 280km from Derby, Over the Range Tyre and Mechanical is the only mechanic along the Gibb; email Nev at overtherangetyres@gmail.com or call (08) 9191 7887. Nev does tyre repairs, offers new and second-hand tyres, and does minor mechanical and welding repairs.

If you are expecting to roll into Broome or Kununurra for a service, you must have booked it months in advance. If you break down in a remote area, it can be very expensive to get you out, so I recommend carrying minor spares (belts, hoses, fluids and the tools needed to replace them) and investing in premium roadside assistance from one of the various state-based motoring clubs, like RAC WA or NRMA.

4WDING AND ROAD SAFETY

Here are four essentials for a happy and safe road trip in the remote areas of the Kimberley:

Prepare your vehicle for remote area driving. I recommend that you check your engine's oil and fluids, carry two spare tyres and, if you don't have long-range tanks but are travelling off-road, multiple jerry cans with enough fuel to get you to the next fuel stop. In addition, carry a well-stocked first-aid kit and the knowledge of how to use it.

Bring plenty of water (up to five litres per person, per day, plus extra in case of a breakdown), and stock up on food before you leave Broome, Derby or Kununurra. Food, especially fresh produce, can be expensive along the Gibb River Road and its offshoots.

Tell someone where you are going and when you expect to be back. Mobile phone reception is almost non-existent on the Gibb River Road and into the Mitchell Plateau. It can be limited between towns on the Great Northern Highway. If you plan to be out of phone range for more than a few days, consider taking or renting a satellite phone or emergency beacon (either an EPIRB, inReach, Spot or similar). If you break down, stay with your vehicle in a shady spot. Don't attempt to walk to safety, as heat exhaustion or hyperthermia can overtake you very quickly in the Kimberley, and if you're with your car you are easier to find.

"Drive slowly and enjoy the scenery – drive fast and join the scenery," said author Douglas Horton. I've seen my fair share of car wrecks along the Gibb River Road, the result of drivers travelling along the corrugations at the same speed as on a highway. Slow down. If others are trying to overtake, pull gently to the left and give them more room.

DRIVING OFF ROAD

With so much of the Kimberley's best bits off-road, the ability to drive onto the sand or down a rough track will separate you from the crowds, helping you find remote campsites and epic waterholes. But, if you haven't done much 4WDing before, it can be daunting. So, to make the most of your time exploring without spending significant parts of it bogged, follow these simple tips.

Let air out of your tyres

Not just some air, let heaps out. If you drive onto a beach with more than 20psi in the tyres, you'll probably get bogged. If you cross the Gibb without reducing tyre pressures, you'll be supporting remote communities by purchasing the most expensive tyres you've ever bought (if you have a blowout, take your old tyre with you and dispose of it responsibly). There is literally no more cost-effective vehicle modification you can make than simply deflating the tyres to suit the conditions.

On beaches, deflate them until the 4WD glides to a gentle stop when you take your foot off the accelerator, rather than lurch to one. That's usually around 15-20psi. If you get bogged, let more air out until you're not. On dirt, depending on load, reduce pressures by 10-15psi and slow down.

Stop before you get bogged

The key to not getting bogged is realising you're about to be. If you can stop the car before the car is stopped, then that leaves you room to wiggle. Once you've stopped, get out and let some air out of your tyres. Then, reverse back a little until you feel your progress restricted, then drive forward a little until you feel the same. All going well, you should be able to repeat this as many times as it takes to bed a firm track under the car, which you can use to gain momentum on and drive out. It might take 15 minutes, but that's easier than two hours of digging.

Wear a seatbelt

Just because you're off-road it doesn't mean you're not responsible for your safety and that of your passengers. It's also a legal requirement to wear a seatbelt on roads and road-related areas in Australia, including beaches.

Watch the tides

If you plan on driving onto any of the Kimberley's beaches, either side of low tide is the best time. That is when the beach is widest, and if you get stuck, you've got the most time to get yourself unstuck before the tide comes back in (when Kimberley tides come in, they come in a long way). Only drive between the low and high tide marks to avoid damaging vegetation and dune systems, and stick to existing tracks, if there are some already.

If you need to turn around, turn downhill

Driving on sand is much easier if you don't have to also drive up a hill. If you need to turn around while you're on the beach and go the other way, start on the high side and finish your turn on the low side, then use momentum to slowly climb back up the beach. If you start on the low side, you'll likely be at your slowest on the steepest part of the turn, and that's when you may get stuck.

PERMITS

Much of the land in the Kimberley is Indigenous, private or government-owned. In many places, you'll need permission or a permit to visit.

National Parks

It costs $15 per vehicle per day to enter the five Kimberley national parks – Purnululu

(Bungle Bungles), Dimalurru (Tunnel Creek), Bandilngan (Windjana Gorge), Mirima, and Wunaamin Conservation Park. If you're planning on visiting them all, it's cheaper to buy a two-week or one-month Holiday Pass ($40 and $60, respectively). An annual All Parks Pass for $120 is good value if you travel long-term. Contact Parks and Wildlife Service on (08) 9219 9000 or via their website shop.dbca.wa.gov.au.

Indigenous Land

To visit Indigenous lands, you must obtain a transit permit, which is free from dplh.wa.gov.au. It could take a few weeks, so plan in advance or chat with the visitor centres in Broome or Kununurra. Some Indigenous communities also require you to pay for visitor permits, and you may need proof of COVID vaccination.

Entry onto Wunambal Gaambera land (for Mitchell Plateau, see page 118) requires an Uunguu Visitor Pass and proof of COVID vaccination. The passes can be obtained easily online and they cost $50 per person, valid for five days (family discounts are available, as are longer passes for bushwalkers). Apply at wunambalgaambera.org.au/shop.

You'll also need a permit to visit Ardyaloon (One Arm Point). That's $18 per adult and $5 for kids 6-16 and includes a guided tour of the trochus hatchery. Get the permits from the community office or the supermarket when you arrive.

VISITOR CENTRES:

The Kimberley's visitor centres are the lifeblood of tourism in the region, and their passionate staff want to show you the best places. Hours of operation can vary, but call them to find out road conditions, to book a tour or just to learn about the region.

Broome Visitor Centre
1 Hamersley Street, Broome – (08) 9195 2200
enquiries@visitbroome.com.au

Derby Visitor Centre
30 Loch Street, Derby
(08) 9191 1426
manager@derbytourism.com.au

Fitzroy Crossing Visitor Centre
5 Flynn Drive, Fitzroy Crossing
(08) 9191 5355
fxtourism@sdwk.wa.gov.au

Halls Creek Visitor Centre
2 Hall St, Halls Creek
(08) 9168 6007
tourism@hcshire.wa.gov.au

Purnululu National Park Visitor Centre
Spring Creek Track,
Purnululu National Park
(08) 9168 7300

Kununurra Visitor Centre
75 Coolibah Drive, Kununurra
(08) 9168 1177
info@visitkununurra.com

Wyndham Tourist Information Centre
(Kimberley Motors)
6 Great Northern Highway, Wyndham
(08) 9161 1281
mail@thelastfrontier.com.au

WALKING IN THE KIMBERLEY

The Kimberley's rugged terrain can make for some challenging trails. There are very few boardwalks and handrails, and many walks involve rock hopping, wading and clambering over boulders. There is often little or no shade, so avoid the midday sun, carry more water than you think you'll need, and wear shoes with good ankle support. A basic first aid kit is also handy.

Days in the Kimberley can get stinking hot, so keeping well hydrated is essential. The amount of water you will need depends on your activity level: 2 litres per adult per day, if you are mostly relaxing and 5-6 litres if you're hiking in the heat. Avoid walking in the middle of the day whenever possible.

CULTURAL RESPECT

Half of the Kimberley's population is Indigenous. Art and language can vary significantly from one community to the next, but if travelling to an Indigenous community, here are a few things to keep in mind:

- Many communities prohibit the carriage of alcohol – please do not take alcohol into dry communities. Not even stored in your car or van.
- Always ask permission before taking someone's photo. If you'd like to photograph a child, ask their parents or guardians.
- Dress respectfully and avoid skimpy swimwear. Covering yourself appropriately is appreciated by community Elders.
- It's a privilege to visit Indigenous communities. You can give back by purchasing food, fuel or arts and crafts directly from them.
- The handicrafts you'll find in the Kimberley are unique to this region: such as carved boab nuts, ochre paintings and carved mother-of-pearl shells. Sadly, in Australia, up to 85% of art sold as Indigenous souvenirs is fake and imported. Support communities by purchasing directly from them and favour handicrafts unique to the communities you visit. For example, if you want a didgeridoo, perhaps it's best to purchase it from Arnhem Land, where it originated.

WHAT TO PACK

Whenever you come, expect the weather to be warmer than you're used to. Bring sun protection, including a hat, toxin-free sunscreen, lightweight, long-sleeved shirts, and swimmers. Dry Season nights can get very cold (0°C isn't uncommon inland), so don't forget to pack some warmer clothes.

You'll need thongs or sandals, plus a sturdy pair of walking/hiking shoes that provide ankle support and grip for rock hopping. Although it's almost always shorts weather, long pants are perfect for longer hikes to protect against the Kimberley's needle-like spinifex grass.

And don't forget your reusable water bottle, coffee cup, and grocery bags to avoid single-use plastics wherever you find yourself.

WHERE TO STAY

Accommodation in the Kimberley is as wild and varied as the countryside. There's everything from $3,000 a night, all-inclusive resorts to simple free camps beside quiet creeks. I've rolled my swag out in most of them.

Throughout this book, I've mentioned some of my favourite campsites, caravan parks, and resorts. If you plan on staying in a caravan park in Broome or Kununurra during the peak of the tourist season (June to August), you will need to make a booking, often months (if not a year) in advance. Especially if you plan on travelling with your dog.

You'll get the most out of your Kimberley experience if you're prepared to rough it under canvas for at least a night or two, but even if you're not, there is no shortage of station stays, safari cabins and bungalows scattered across the Kimberley, and even in the more remote areas.

CARING FOR THE KIMBERLEY

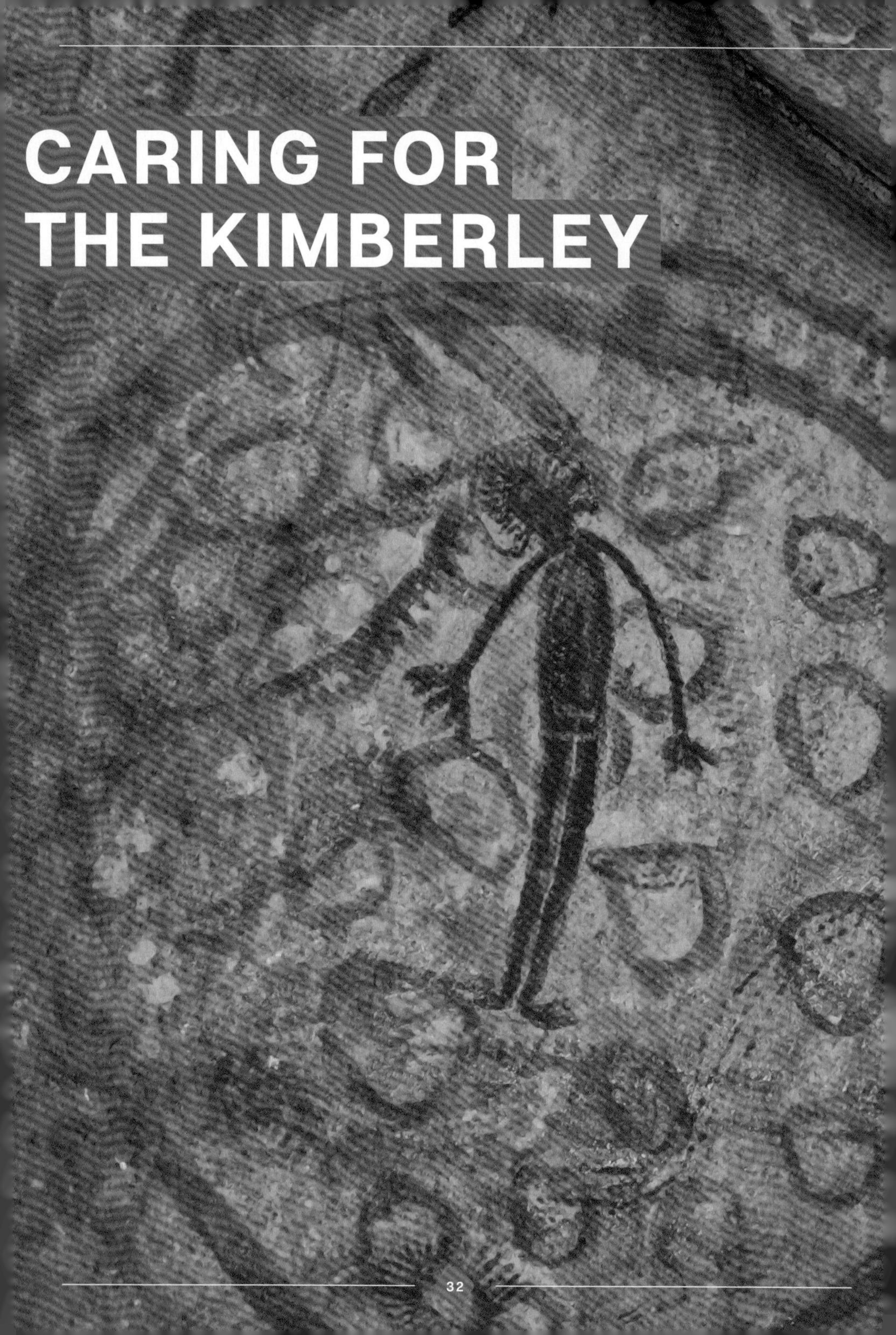

CARING FOR COUNTRY

Leave it better than you found it

"You've written a beautiful piece, but they closed that waterhole to tourists shortly after they opened it, as people left rubbish and soiled the waters with sunscreen and shampoo. The rock painting sites became a similar issue with people touching and destroying artworks".

– Email received from a Traditional Owner, which resulted in me pulling an incredible waterhole out of this book at the last minute.

As you can see from this email, when a place gets trashed, it affects us all. The aim should always be to leave it better than you found it. So please pick up any rubbish you find lying around and hold onto it until it can be responsibly disposed of. In just about all of the remote communities and campsites across the Kimberley, there is no effective or efficient rubbish disposal system. Please come prepared to take out everything you bring in (this includes toilet paper - don't leave it in the bush or bury it). Anything you don't will eventually be washed into the waterways during the Wet Season.

Outback Cleanups

If you're passionate about keeping the outback clean, consider supporting the work of the non-profit Outback Cleanups Australia - outbackcleanupsaustralia.com. Run by legends Boe and Kim, they have removed, collected, recycled, and data logged 67,300kg of rubbish pollution from remote beach, bush and marine environments in Australia since 2019.

CARING FOR PEOPLE

Kimberley Spirit Foundation

While many visitors idealise what it must be like to live in the Kimberley, the truth is, alongside the incredible lifestyle, there are some real challenges. The Kimberley is an isolated region with the highest rate of Indigenous youth suicide in the nation.

It was after a friend of mine, who I went to school with in Broome, took his own life that I founded the Kimberley Spirit Foundation, together with six other board members. Right now, our work involves cooking and delivering nutritious meals to children in need, one night a week. These meals are cooked by myself and my wife, Taminga (while we also look after six children) and hand-delivered by ourselves, or volunteers, into the local community. Our future goal is to increase this food delivery to at least two nights per week and to develop youth programs around watersports and tourism-related job pathways.

In the beautiful Kimberley region, where sexual and substance abuse; poor health and nutrition; and lack of connection with local employment opportunities have contributed to a cycle of poverty and hopelessness amongst some of our Indigenous people, the Kimberley Spirit Foundation has a vision to help reduce youth suicide and empower the next generation to thrive, not just survive. *It's about LiViN'* - that's our motto.

We currently exist from private donations, so if this cause resonates with you, please see kimberleyspirit.com/ksfoundation, where you can donate or sign up for our newsletter.

CLEVELAND
23
WORLDWIDE

INDIGENOUS ART GUIDE

INDIGENOUS ART CENTRES

There are many talented Indigenous artists in the Kimberley. My wife, Taminga, is one of them. The best way to support local artists is to buy directly from them or an Indigenous-owned gallery. Here are a few that I recommend:

Kimberley Spirit Arthouse, Kununurra

I hope you don't mind if I start with my number one favourite Kimberley artist, my gorgeous wife, Taminga Connell (pictured to the left). Taminga is a Bunaba/Kija woman with connection to the Jaru and Ngarinyin people. Her contemporary paintings tell stories of her childhood and family, spirituality, unity amongst all people and cultures, dreams and connection. For an appointment to view the Kimberley Spirit Arthouse or her artworks, visit kimberleyspirit.com/taminga.

Waringarri Aboriginal Arts, Kununurra

Established in the 1980s, Waringarri is the first wholly Indigenous-owned art centre established in Western Australia, and one of the oldest, continuously-operating art centres in Australia. You can find it opposite the turn-off to Kelly's Knob (page 144). Walk through the Dawang gallery, see artists at work, or join one of their cultural tours encompassing art, music and bush tucker. See waringarriarts.com.au

Warmun Art Centre, Warmun Community

On the Great Northern Highway, 53km north from the turn-off to Purnululu (the Bungle Bungles), the community of Warmun is world-renowned for its art centre and the artists' unique style of painting with ochres (earth pigments) and uncluttered compositions. Call ahead to ensure they'll be open for your visit. Phone (08) 9168 7496 or visit warmunart.com.au.

Mangkaja Arts Resource Agency, Fitzroy Crossing

Mangkaja represents artists across four language groups within the Fitzroy Valley region. The space serves as an art gallery and a studio for artists. The art here is known for its vibrant colours, and the artists also create baskets, carvings and traditional artefacts. Visit mangkaja.com

Marnin Studio, Fitzroy Crossing

'Marnin' means women in the Walmajarri language. A social enterprise of the Marninwarntikura Women's Resource Centre, the studio is a therapeutic healing space for local Bunuba, Gooniyandi, Wankatjunka, Walmajarri and Nykina women. Apart from paintings, there is also a terrific range of homewares including cushions, naturally dyed silk scarves and block-printed textiles. marninstudio.com.au.

Mowanjum Art and Culture Centre, Mowanjum Community

Travelling east just 3km after the turn-off down the Gibb River Road, you'll find Mowanjum's community and the iconic art centre built in the shape of a giant Wandjina head. This is the creative epicentre for the Worrorra, Ngarinyin and Wunumbal tribes, who are the custodians of Wandjina law and iconography. I recommend coming during the annual Mowanjum Festival, usually held each July. See mowanjumarts.com.

Nagula Jarndu Designs, Broome

Yawuru Jarndu started operating in 1987 as an Indigenous women's resource centre. It currently has a membership of 120 Indigenous women, with seven Yawuru women who are the directors. Its aim was to record oral history and preserve Yawuru culture. Lovely screen prints and textiles are available at the retail outlet called Nagula Jarndu Designs. See nagulajarndu.com.au.

Kira Kiro Art Centre, Kalumburu

Kira Kiro is the local word for Bradshaw figures, as seen on the rock faces of caves throughout this region. The Kira Kiro dominate the iconography of many modern paintings on paper and canvas coming out of this art centre, located on the land of the Kwini people in Kalumburu.
See facebook.com/kirakiroartists

Kalumburu Strong Women's Art Collective, Kalumburu

This micro-enterprise was established in 2018 to empower and provide financial support to the women of the Kalumburu community. The ladies sell a range of beautiful artworks, including acrylics on canvas, prints and a range of homewares and textiles. If you can't make it up to Kalumburu, there is a fantastic online shop. kalumburustrongwomensartcollective.org.

ROCK ART

There are two distinctive rock art styles in the Kimberley; Wandjina and Gwion Gwion (or Bradshaw).

Wandjina art (pictured to the right) is unmistakable and iconic, characterised by round, mouthless faces with large, vacant eyes and halos which are believed to represent clouds. The Worrorra, Ngarinyin and Wunambal tribes are the custodians of Wandjina law and iconography.

The Gwion Gwion figures (also known as Kira Kiro or Bradshaw) are vastly different. As seen below, they are characterised by elegantly depicted long bodies, often adorned with tassels, bags and headdresses. Gwion Gwion art is believed to be the oldest figurative art in the world – older than the pyramids of Egypt!

Both types of rock art are scattered throughout the Kimberley, however, the greatest rock art panels I've encountered are within a few kilometres of the coast.

BROOME AND THE DAMPIER PENINSULA

Broome represents something different to everyone that spends time here. To the tourist, it's a means to escape winter down south for sunny days and warm ocean swims. For the city dweller, it swaps traffic lights and concrete for empty roads and colourful coastlines.

For local people, Broome is a deliberate choice – one of swimming, fishing and camping instead of shopping malls and high rises.

Broome is a transient town; many come for a few years before the remote lifestyle proves too much. It's 2,000km from the nearest city, and the harsh Wet Seasons, expensive food, and limited supplies take their toll. Like the tourists, many residents get a taste, relax for a while, then depart, changed, with dreams of returning for future holidays.

But the remote lifestyle has its obvious perks, too, like endless opportunities for adventure down red dirt tracks and super starry nights because there's no light pollution.

Broome is where I grew up through the 1990s. I attended Broome Primary and High School before moving to my current home of Kununurra. The '90s was a real crossover period for Broome, with Ansett the only airline carrier flying from the east coast and tourism still finding its feet. Everyone shopped at Charlie Carters near Town Beach, and there was just a tiny kiosk at Cable Beach selling milkshakes and sandwiches. Broome's identity was rapidly morphing from pearling port to tourism town (and a fly-in/fly-out point for workers on nearby mines).

Bardi Elder, Bruce Wiggan, with his Riji (traditionally carved pearl shell) at Cygnet Bay Pearl Farm

Given how remote Broome is, when visitors discover Chinatown is the central shopping district (and other surprises like the Japanese cemetery), they are surprised by how multicultural the town is. Of course, it all makes sense if you've read about Broome's pearling history (I recommend visiting Broome Museum, see page 53). During its pearling heyday, the town must've been wild; pearl luggers lined the foreshore and, in Chinatown, you could buy tasty Asian food or visit a billiard saloon, brothel, or opium den.

But long before the arrival of the luggers, the Indigenous Yawuru people thrived on this country and hunted its waters. In fact, the townsite of Broome was established near three native waterholes in Roebuck Bay. These days, to visit Broome without experiencing Yawuru culture with an Indigenous guide would be to skim the surface.

It's the same on Ardi (the Dampier Peninsula), north of Broome, where you'll get the opportunity to camp on Indigenous land and learn about the traditional way of life, which involves plenty of hunting and gathering in simple harmony with the land. Although Cape Leveque's red dirt road is now sealed, and the peninsula has become much more accessible, the phone reception is still patchy. Here's a place to turn off your phone and slow down to Peninsula time. Plus, the fishing, camping and beach exploring up here are phenomenal.

For those who can relax into a laidback lifestyle (and realise that the little makeshift campsite reception area may be unattended until the local family returns from mud crabbing), a visit to Broome and Ardi will be one of the most enriching life experiences you can have.

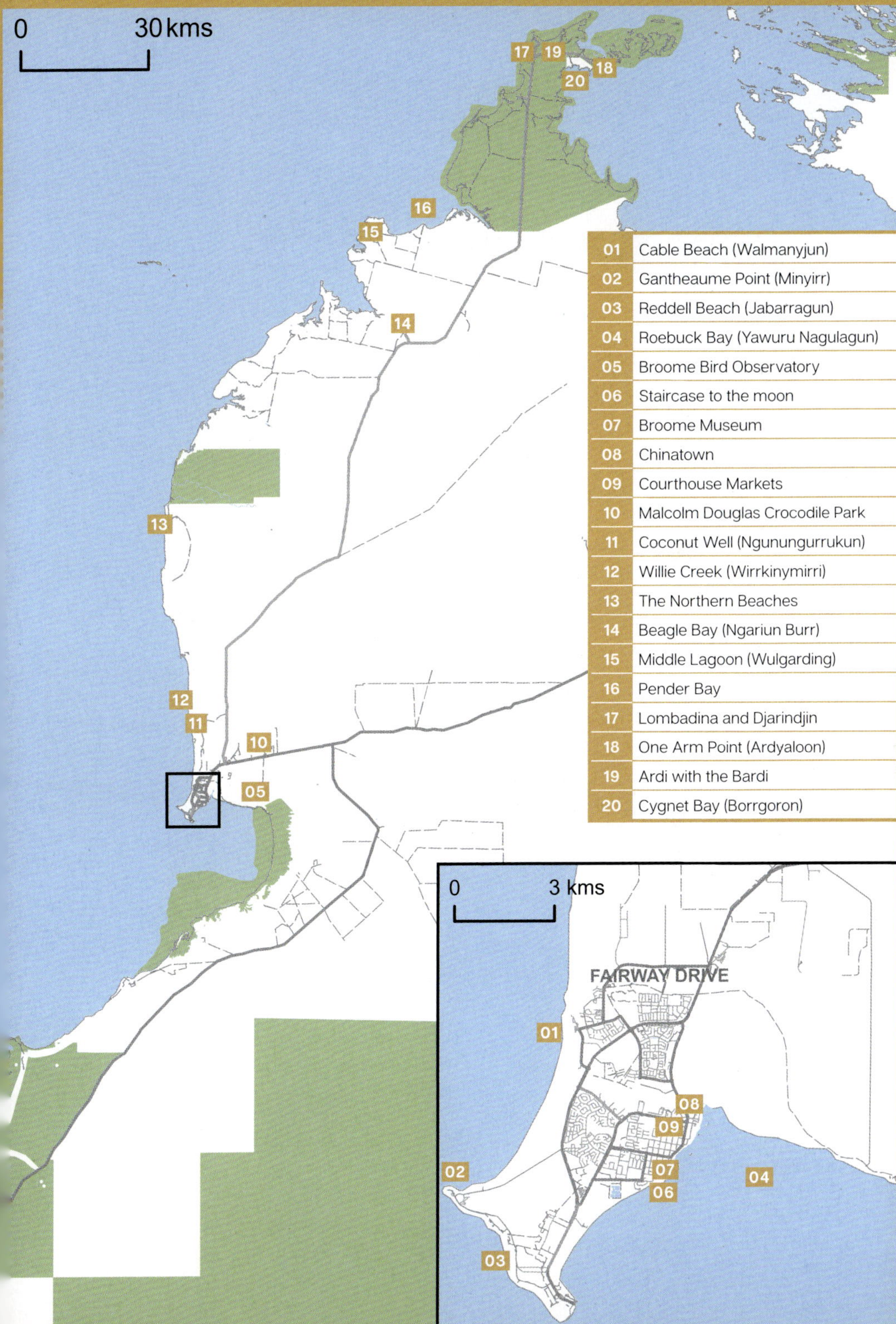

0 30 kms
01 Cable Beach (Walmanyjun)
02 Gantheaume Point (Minyirr)
03 Reddell Beach (Jabarragun)
04 Roebuck Bay (Yawuru Nagulagun)
05 Broome Bird Observatory
06 Staircase to the moon
07 Broome Museum
08 Chinatown
09 Courthouse Markets
10 Malcolm Douglas Crocodile Park
11 Coconut Well (Ngunungurrukun)
12 Willie Creek (Wirrkinymirri)
13 The Northern Beaches
14 Beagle Bay (Ngariun Burr)
15 Middle Lagoon (Wulgarding)
16 Pender Bay
17 Lombadina and Djarindjin
18 One Arm Point (Ardyaloon)
19 Ardi with the Bardi
20 Cygnet Bay (Borrgoron)
0 3 kms
FAIRWAY DRIVE

CABLE BEACH (WALMANYJUN) 1/100 ☐

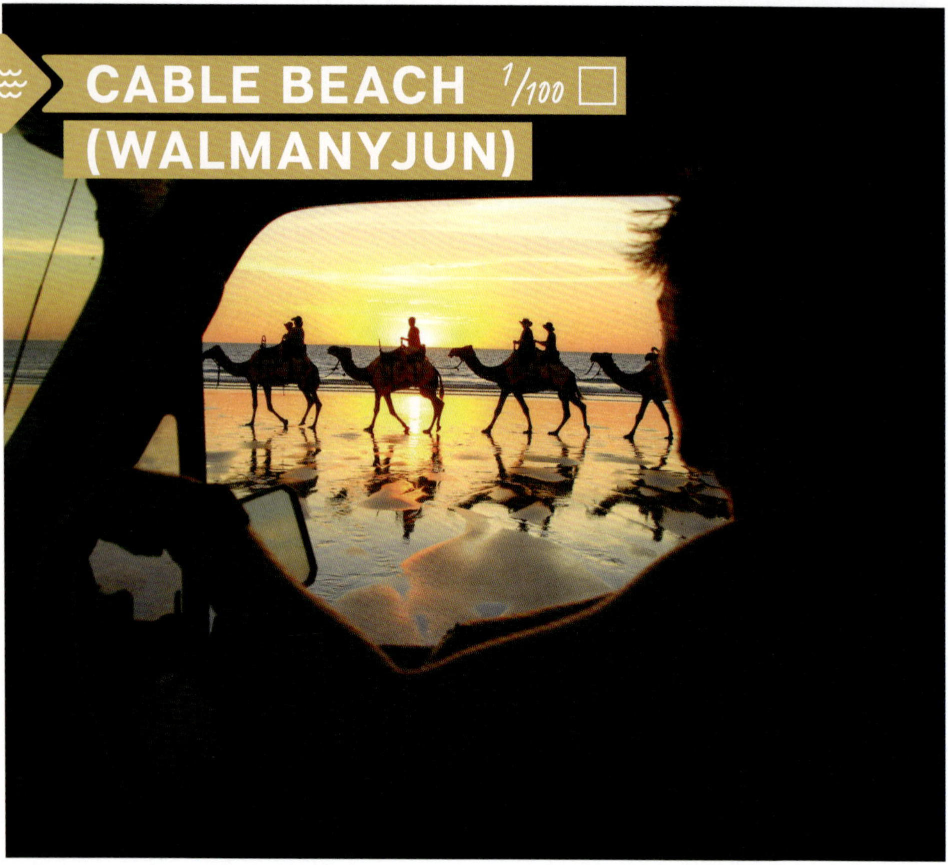

White sand, turquoise sea and a nudie beach

Few rituals are more sacred than watching the sunset at Cable Beach. Each afternoon of the Dry Season, tourists and locals perch their camping chairs on the grassy knoll above Cable Beach, munching cheese and crackers, watching for the elusive 'green flash' in the final seconds before the sun disappears over the horizon. Those in the know head up the stairs to the left of Zanders restaurant, where it's less crowded, or to the surf club, which offers cool bevvies and a local atmosphere (Thursday to Sunday, 4 pm to 8.30 pm).

If you'd rather spend your sunset on the sand, setting up north of the rocks visible from the main carpark is popular. You can jump on a camel (book at least a week in advance) or pick a spot and wait for them to walk past to nail that quintessential sunset shot.

Known as Walmanyjun in the local Yawuru language, the name Cable Beach was given in 1889 after an undersea telegraph cable was laid between Broome and Java. And all these years later, little has changed along this 22km stretch of sand with a refreshing lack of development.

There are plenty of ways to enjoy the beach: walk 7km from Cables south to Gantheaume at sunrise and then catch the

7.57 am bus back to town (bebus.com.au). Rent an umbrella or a paddle board from Darrell at the Beach Hut. Or hire a jet ski from Ultimate Watersports.

If you've got a 4WD, you can drive along the sand north of the rocks to Coconut Well (page 58) and Willie Creek. The whole stretch is a designated nudist beach, so you could enjoy some nudie bathing along the way. Be sure to pack your board for the occasional surfable wave on the stretch between the main area of Cable Beach and Coconut Well (the rocky areas of the main beach are usually your best bet for a wave). Check the tide before taking your vehicle onto the beach – the Kimberley has the world's largest tropical tidal range, and I've seen a few cars get swallowed over the years. For the future enjoyment of all, reduce your speed around people and don't drive in the dunes, especially in flatback turtle nesting season (November to February), when beach driving is restricted anyway.

Cable Beach is generally considered safe to swim, but there are risks. Box jellyfish and the deadly Irukandji (irra-can-gee) appear sporadically between November and May, so read the signs before jumping into the water during the stinger season. In recent years, sharks and salties have also become a menace, though their sightings are rare. Swimming between the Surf Lifesaver flags is always the safest option. When the occasional saltie appears, Broome Shire is always quick to react, closing the beach for 24 hours and catching any rogue crocs. Still, if the occasional saltie sighting concerns you, opt for one of the rockpools at Gantheaume Point or Coconut Well instead.

01

02

01 Surfers are often surprised to find that Cable Beach is (sometimes) surfable

02 On a low tide, you can drive north from Cable Beach to Coconut Well

GANTHEAUME POINT (MINYIRR) 2/100 ☐

Rockpool heaven

At the southern end of Cable Beach is Gantheaume Point (Minyirr). Here you'll find an ugly, steel-framed lighthouse set amongst a desert-meets-sea landscape. You can often see migrating whales, turtles and manta rays from the rocks.

You can see dinosaur footprints at the base of the rocky cliffs beyond the lighthouse on a king low tide. Otherwise, there are concrete castings up near the lighthouse. Come on an 8+ metre tide, and you'll find some idyllic rockpools freshly topped up by the sea. During my school years in Broome, Anastasia's Pool was a favourite (hand-built in the 1920s by Patrick Percy for his wife, Anastasia, to help soothe her arthritis), but this rockpool got ruined by bad weather in 2014. Nevertheless, there are still some great little pools to be found after a high tide by walking down the lighthouse track and exploring the rocks. To get amongst the marine action, join Broome Adventure Co. for their three-hour 'turtle kayak' from $90 per person. broomeadventure.com.au.

If you time your visit for sunset, get your camera ready for the cliffs to light up as the sun sinks into the sea. Magic. Just north of the lighthouse, you can drive onto the beach (enter opposite the racecourse), which is the far southern end of Cable Beach. This spot gets packed at sunset.

Minyirr is a spiritually significant place to the Yawuru people, as it's their Dreamtime birthplace. The Yawuru are happy to share their knowledge of plants, animals, bush medicines and Dreamtime stories on one of their walking tours. Call Minyirr Park's office to arrange on (08) 9194 0150. Adults are $35, and kids are $9. If you're after a longer walk, Minyirr marks the beginning of the Lurujarri Heritage Trail, a nine-day walk along an ancient songline with the Goolarabooloo people – goolarabooloo.org.au.

REDDELL BEACH (JABARRAGUN) 3/100 ☐

A hidden, red-cliffed beach in Broome

Captain John Reddell and his son sadly met their demise during an onboard mutiny after he sailed his pearling lugger, Ethel, out of Broome in 1899. But his name lives on at Reddell Beach (mistakenly spelt Riddell on Google maps). The scenery is remarkable, with red cliffs weathered by cyclones and tides into intriguing shapes and patterns, beautifully contrasting with the turquoise Indian Ocean.

It's a place where locals walk their dogs and, being a little off the beaten track (a 4WD vehicle is recommended for the sometimes-boggy dirt track), there are usually only a handful of people enjoying this stretch of sand. Though, that could change soon with the Australian government, in late 2020, pledging $800,000 to develop the area, potentially adding bus parking. Follow the updates or join the conversation on the Facebook group 'Reddell Beach Lovers'.

To get to Reddell Beach, drive down the red, unsealed Kavite Road between Broome's Port and Gantheaume Point and then turn into carpark three to find the rough walking trail down onto the beach via the craggy coastal cliffs. Like the other Broome beaches, you'll enjoy endless, blue-sky days from May to October. However, jellyfish can appear between November to May (look for warning signs), and you'll need to be wary of strong currents; there are no lifeguards on duty here.

ROEBUCK BAY 4/100 ☐ (YAWURU NAGULAGUN)

Dinosaurs, dolphins and flying boats

Declared a marine park in 2015, Roebuck Bay (or Yawuru Nagulagun, meaning 'sea country of the Yawuru people') lies south of Cable Beach on the eastern side of Broome's peninsula. The two coastal stretches couldn't be any more different.

Mangroves, mudflats and pindan cliffs characterise the bay. If you visit the red-cliffed beach just north of Town Beach (Guwarri) on an outgoing high tide, you'll see the 'pindan tides', where the red dirt mixes with the turquoise sea. It looks like a painting, with colours too vivid to be real!

Roebuck Bay is the vantage point to see Broome's most famous natural phenomenon, Staircase to the Moon (see page 52). The bay is also the place to view ancient theropod and sauropod dinosaur footprints. For the Yawuru people, the three-toed tracks of the Megalosauropus broomensis belonged to Marala, who came to instil rule and law to the land. But Megalorsauropus wasn't the only one to have walked this land in ancient times, with 21 types of dinosaur prints having now been discovered over 100km of coastline – something you won't find anywhere else in the world.

The Colless family are long-time Broome locals who offer fantastic, guided tours to check out the footprints from their shaded, flat-bottom boat. They deliver punters right into the action and provide fascinating commentary. Check out broomehovercraft.com.au or phone (08) 9193 5025 for current tour times.

Not many folks know this, but during WWII, Broome was bombed by Japanese Zeros, and you can still see the wrecks of six of the Dornier and Catalina Flying Boats on a king low tide in Roebuck Bay. You can either walk through sticky mud for about 1.5km or, alternatively, jump onto a three-hour tour with the Colless family.

If you're a bird enthusiast, this is the place to see migratory birds flock here by the thousands. The birds come to feed amongst the nutrient-rich tidal flats and roost on the beaches. The Bird Observatory is on the eastern side of Roebuck Bay and it offers great camping. Another creature that can be spotted in the bay is the snubfin dolphin. Roebuck is home to Australia's largest known population of snubfins, which are regularly seen swimming and playing in the turquoise waters. The bay is rich in seagrass, a dietary staple for the dolphins and other marine creatures.

01 A snubfin dolphin

02 Crab Creek (Mangalagun)

02

BROOME BIRD OBSERVATORY 5/100 □

This great campsite flies under the radar

I love birds and, like many Kimberley locals, can rattle off the names of a few. I wouldn't say I'm a full-blown twitcher, but I love seeing a pair of brolgas in the bush, or a rainbow bee-eater swooping in front whilst relaxing in a gorge, or being able to identify the sound of a bird and know what it is before I even see it. The Kimberley is wild, and the more you tune into the wild, the greater the experience you'll have.

There's an amazing campsite just half an hour out of Broome that flies under the radar despite receiving over 100,000 visitors each season. These winged visitors are a spectacle to behold as clouds of feathers fill the skies over Roebuck Bay. The bay is a Ramsar-listed wetland and one of the world's best bird-watching spots. To date, 333 bird species (a third of Australia's total birds) have been recorded in Broome. Their presence is spectacular.

Broome Bird Observatory was set up in 1988, and it's largely run by passionate volunteers. Though the birds are the main event, this is also a great spot just to retreat in nature; to stargaze at night with very low light pollution, to go bushwalking or fishing, or to look for dinosaur footprints. Whether you're a committed twitcher or a newbie to the birdie scene, the Observatory runs some great tours, such as its 2.5-hour shorebird tour at $80 per person. In 2021, it completed its four-year build of a discovery centre, which is $10 per adult, free for those under 16 and only $8 if you stay overnight. Remember, this is a research and education facility, and all your silvers go to the cause of bird conservation and science.

BBO's accommodation is rustic but clean and comfortable (thanks to the camp volunteers). It beats packing in like sardines at the campsites of Broome. The sites are small and narrow, suitable for tents, swags or caravans under 16 feet. The camp kitchen is where everyone comes together each night for Bird Log, a ritual that's been happening for three decades. This is a social event, but it's also essential for data collection of bird species spotted by visitors, wardens and volunteers.

There are decent bathroom facilities (including hot showers), and it's not uncommon to find a green tree frog staring up at you from inside the toilet, something that I'm personally used to from the outdoor bathroom in my Kununurra home. It's priced well at $20 per person, per night (adult), $10 for kids 8-12, or under eight are free. Campsites are unpowered, and, sorry, no dogs. Despite the proximity to Broome, mobile reception is sketchy, if at all. Switching off your phone is your best bet, so you can tune in to nature. Switching to twitching! There are also basic units, where a single room will set you back $45 a night, or a double or family room $85 a night. A bargain, I say, especially given the incredible location.

STAIRCASE TO THE MOON

6/100 ☐

A shimmering staircase reflected from a rising full moon

What exactly is the staircase to the moon? Well, imagine that the low tide has retreated, and there are puddles of water on the tidal flats. A full moon rises across the bay, and as it does, the pools reflect its light and a staircase effect is created. It's so clear it seems like you could walk up it.

Similar effects can be seen on other water bodies around the northwest, but the Kimberley's huge tides and dark nights make this natural phenomenon especially spectacular.

The best viewing spots are the Mangrove Hotel and Town Beach (Guwarri), where popular night markets are held when the full moon rises from April to October. So bring your picnic rug, grab some tucker from the food vans and enjoy one of nature's true wonders.

If you are travelling south, there are other staircases at Hearsons Cove near Karratha, Onslow (306km south of Karratha), Reader's Head at Cossack, and Port Hedland too.

BROOME MUSEUM 7/100

A little museum with big stories

Do you know much about the Broome bombings during WWII? Or that it was once considered the pearling capital of the world? Thankfully, back in the '70s, as some important historical objects were being discarded, Jean Haynes (nee Kennedy) and some other concerned locals set up the historical society. Without their efforts, some vital pieces of Broome's history may have been lost.

Though small, Broome's museum is a must-visit for anyone keen on diving into its bygone era. I recommend dropping in as soon as you arrive in Broome, as you'll experience the town differently, knowing its history.

Located near Town Beach (Guwarri) in old Broome and run by volunteers, this non-profit museum is spread across three historical buildings. The main was a general store built in the 1890s. It became Customs House in 1910 and then the museum in 1981. Inside, you'll find fascinating information about the March 1942 air attacks on Broome by Japanese Zero planes as well as Broome's pearling, paleontological and Indigenous Yawuru history.

The Sailmaker's Shed is a wonderful new addition to the museum. It was built in 1897 for Charles Bagge's sailmaking business and was recently restored by the historical society after a demolition order had been placed on it. Charles was a Swedish sailmaker during Broome's pearling heyday, and the various displays within this shed are super interesting to walk through.

A visit to Broome Museum will set you back a reasonable $12 per adult and nothing for kids under 16. Opening hours are 10 am to 4 pm Monday to Friday and 10 am to 1 pm on weekends and daily between May and September, or 10 am to 1 pm from October to April. broomemuseum.org.au

CHINATOWN 8/100 ☐

The historical heart of Broome

Today's Chinatown is an eclectic mix of cafes, art galleries and pearl shops, but this historic part of Broome once resembled a scene from a wild west movie. Pearl luggers lined the foreshore, and Chinatown was entertainment central with Chinese eateries, bazaars, billiard saloons and brothels. Walking Chinatown's 1.2km Heritage Trail, you'll discover historic buildings and remnants of yesteryear, especially from the town's pearling heyday.

Don't miss out on watching a movie from a deckchair at the world's oldest open-air picture gardens – Sun Pictures. It's located smack bang in the middle of Chinatown. Sun Pictures opened its doors in 1916 during the silent movie era. Since then, it's survived some challenging times, including attacks from Japanese Zeros and racially segregated seating. Before the levee bank was built in Chinatown in 1974, king tides flooded the theatre. Some folks claimed that it was possible to catch a fish during screenings! During the day, the doors stay open, so you can wander in and suss out the old memorabilia. broomemovies.com.au.

Across on Dampier Terrace, you'll find Streeter's Jetty, which was used by pearling luggers when Broome was the pearling capital of the world. Built initially for pearl dealer and merchant E. W. Streeter and Co. of London in the late 1890s, it's now the only remaining jetty used by luggers to offload Mother of Pearl. The timber jetty extends into the mangroves with the original iron tram tracks in the mud below. The tramway that linked the jetty with Chinatown was in operation until 1948. After you've seen the jetty, continue walking down Dampier Terrace, and you'll find the Pearl Luggers Museum opposite the historic Roebuck Bay Hotel. Check out the old hard hat diving suits, listen to pearler's tales of the old days and see the Sam Male, a restored pearling lugger.

While in Chinatown, grab a bite because some of Broome's best tucker can be found here. I recommend the Short St. Cafe, owned by my mate and one of the Kimberley's original photography gurus, Yane Sotiroski. Try The Good Cartel or The Aarli for dinner and Land of Pharaohs anytime, near Coles, for all the goodness.

COURTHOUSE MARKETS 9/100 ☐

Food and handicrafts in the gardens of Broome's historic Courthouse

Doughnuts, homemade ice cream and frozen mango fruit-things are some of the tasty treats that await you at Broome's weekend markets in the Courthouse's heritage-listed gardens. Open year-round between 8 am and 1 pm on Saturdays and Sunday mornings from April to October, the small but packed-with-local-goodness Courthouse Markets is a great place to gather with mates, meet locals and enjoy the flavours of Broome. If you're flying out of Broome in the afternoon and need a few hours to fill after check-out, spend the morning here; it's near the airport.

I recommend skipping your hotel breakfast and filling up on goodness at the market, but prepare for a line-up at some stalls, especially the coffee stand. For lunch, don't miss Maryani's satays at the Indonesian caravan, served with a sauce that's been a hit for more than 25 years. Another must-munch is the fresh, hot doughnuts that Les serves up at his doughnut van. To enjoy your tucker like locals, bring a picnic rug and relax on the lawn under shady trees in the courtyard grounds.

For some locally-made gifts, Hidden Valley Handcrafts sells a gorgeous range of natural soaps, candles and skin lotions. Its 'midgie magic' salve is perfect for sandfly bites. There's also a great selection of affordable pearls amongst the market's jewellery stalls. One thing's for sure; it's impossible to walk out of the Courthouse Markets empty-handed!

If night markets are more your scene, there's one held at Town Beach (Guwarri) each Thursday from June to September. And if you're lucky enough to be in Broome during the Staircase to the Moon (page 52), there's the Staircase Market, also at Town Beach, where you can watch the moonrise, grab some tucker and suss out the various handicrafts on offer.

EAT

Broome's early pearling industry lured many Asian workers, and their influence on the local culinary scene is still strong today.

The restaurants and markets have a variety of dishes on offer, and there's also great local seafood, including pearl meat. Beyond the restaurants and cafes, there's plenty of nutritious bush tucker to be picked in season (like boab nuts) and fresh fish to be caught. Here are a few of my favourite eateries:

MATSOS BROOME BREWERY

Matsos' mango and ginger beers are delicious, and the brewery restaurant is open for lunch and dinner with awesome views across Roebuck Bay (pre-book a table on the verandah). This microbrewery is set within a historic (1910) building, and in the shady courtyard out the back, you can listen to live music each afternoon between Friday and Sunday of the Dry Season. There's also an Indian Curry Hut in their courtyard, open seven days during the Dry Season. matsos.com.au.

GINREAB THAI

For Authentic Thai food in Chinatown with fresh ingredients and friendly staff, Ginreab is an absolute winner. Order ahead for takeaway (this spot is popular), and grab some spring rolls, fish cakes, and pad Thai (my recommendations), then head to the beach to enjoy. See the menu at ginreabthai.com.au. Alternatively, another great option nearby is Indonesian restaurant DMK The Kitchen, for Balinese fusion goodness. dmkthekitchen.com.au

THE MANGO PLACE

4km past Malcolm Douglas Crocodile Park on the drive out of Broome is The Mango Place at 12 Mile. Open during the Dry Season, its woodfired pizzas and mango smoothies are delectable, and they have a great range of mango products, like mango wine and chutney. Pretty much everything on the menu has mango in it (did someone say beef and mango pie?) Yum. themangoplace.com.au

MALCOLM DOUGLAS CROCODILE PARK 10/100

The legacy of Malcolm Douglas lives on at Broome's croc park

I deliberated over whether to include this in the book, as it's a very touristy experience and packs a crowd during the season. However, Malcolm Douglas was my old neighbour (from back in the day when the croc park was next to Divers Tavern in Cable Beach) and a legend of the Aussie bush. He was a much-loved Broome local who inspired many (including myself) through his documented adventures with his faithful hound, Boondie. Plus, this may be your only chance to get close to a saltie in the Kimberley. Sadly, Malcolm tragically passed away in 2010 while working at this croc park and animal refuge. Thankfully, the Douglas family has kept it open for the public to enjoy, although now it's 16km out of Broome on Broome Road.

The best (and perhaps busiest) to visit is during the 3 pm croc feeding time. The fun begins as soon as you walk into the park through the giant fibreglass jaws of a saltwater crocodile. Some of the largest crocodiles in captivity in Australia can be found here and, incredibly, are all living together. Apart from crocs and American alligators, there are snakes, lizards, dingoes, and many different bird species, including a cassowary. The croc park is open every day but Christmas from 2 pm to 5 pm. Adults are $35, kids 5-15 are $20, and it's $30 for concession-card holders or $90 for a family of two adults and two kids.

COCONUT WELL 11/100 ☐ (NGUNUNGKURRUKUN)

Rockpools and a blue lagoon

Known to the Yawuru people as Ngunungkurrukun, Coconut Well is a small, beachside community 20km north of Broome. During spring tides, water spills through a gap in the sand dunes creating a stunning lagoon that disappears again as the tide recedes. Bring a pool float so you can ride the tide from the gap in the dunes into the lagoon. It's best on a 10+ metre tide.

Arrive on a low tide to explore what we call the aquariums. If you walk to the limestone, rocky outcrop on the beach just north of the lagoon, you'll find hundreds of rockpools with colourful fish, turtles, and octopuses trapped by the rapidly receding tide. Most of the rockpools are too small to swim in, but I've found a great one on the southern end of the outcrop that's deep enough to plunge into. Just be wary of the limestone, as it's razor-sharp on the hands and feet.

Coconut Well is prime birdie habitat for species such as egret, brolga and jabiru, which feed on the mullet and salmon in the estuary. May to September is your best bet for spotting them.

To get here, turn west off Cape Leveque Road onto McGuigan Road, which becomes Lawrence Road, then turn left onto Denham Road and follow it to the end where there's a small carpark. If you're following Google maps, the suburb may appear as Waterbank. Alternatively, you can beach drive from the rocks at Cable Beach on the low tide, but be weary as the sand may become boggy in parts. People have lost vehicles to the tide in the past.

As always, help keep this area clean and pristine; take your rubbish with you and pick up any you see. If you want a few nights here, which I highly recommend, check out Sol BnB's earth house and glamping bell tents, owned by Broome boy and my old schoolmate, Tao (tell him I sent ya!). See instagram.com/sol.bnb. Alternatively, try Coconutz Bed & Breakfast. coconutz.com.au.

01 Limestone beach pools become aquariums every low tide

02 The ocean fills the lagoon on a 10+ metre tide

03 The carpark next to the lagoon, at the end of Denham Road

04 Glamping at Sol BnB

WILLIE CREEK 12/100 ☐ (WIRRKINYMIRRI)

A tidal estuary and a pearl farm

Drive along the sand north of the rocks at Cable Beach, continue past Coconut Well, and you'll discover the stunning, protected tidal estuary at the mouth of Wirrkinymirri, or Willie Creek. This is a fantastic place to beachcomb or throw in a line for trevally, queenfish and mangrove Jack. You may even spot a sea eagle circling overhead for fish, if you look up. Wirrkinymirri is also a popular beach camping spot for fishing enthusiasts (page 63).

The ocean here is stunning, but interestingly the water colour changes throughout the year. The water is deep blue during the colder months, from May to August. During the warmer months, it's more turquoise. Although the water is alluring, this is not the spot to swim laps – there are a couple of resident saltwater crocs. Older Broome locals still recant the story of a certain leggy Aussie supermodel who swam in the creek's lagoon, oblivious to the fact that she was sharing it with a huge salty which was later spotted by a pilot. It was one 'elle of a close call!

The sparkling waters of Willie Creek are also home to Willie Creek Pearl Farm, where you can learn about farming cultured pearls on a guided tour. williecreekpearls.com.au. The pearl farm offers a unique insight into the history of pearling in the Kimberley and specifically about how the Australian South Sea pearl is farmed from the rare Pinctada maxima shell – the largest of all pearl oysters. The pearl farm is a 38km drive north of Broome via road (take the Cape Leveque turn-off from the Broome Highway, then turn left onto Manari Road and left again onto Willie Creek Road). You can self-drive (4WD recommended) or join a coach from town. There's an option to pre-book lunch for $35, which is a tasty feed and gives you a chance to try pearl meat (alternatively, you can buy pearl meat from Cygnet Bay Pearl Farm's Chinatown showroom). The three-hour self-drive tour costs $79 per adult / $67 per concession / $42 per child, or $200 for two adults and two kids. If you're planning on joining the coach from Broome, then add $50 per adult.

01 During the Wet Season, the water colour turns turquoise

02 One of Willie Creek's resident salties

THE NORTHERN BEACHES 13/100

Fishing and free camping on the beaches north of Broome

The red-cliff beaches of Cape Leveque are well known, but much closer to Broome are what the locals call the Northern Beaches, accessed via the bumpy, unsealed Manari Road (turn left 14km along Cape Leveque Road north of Broome). The beauty here is that it remains wild and rugged. Many creatures call it home, including reptiles, brolga, and endangered bilby. Nesting sea turtles visit the area, and humpbacks migrate past seasonally (August is prime time). There are significant Indigenous cultural heritage sites, and you might also spot dinosaur footprints in the intertidal zone.

As young fellas, my mates and I came up here on weekends with our swags and fishing gear to escape Broome's Dry Season crowds. Although the Northern Beaches are now more well-known, the lack of facilities and the rough tracks deter most. Getting to the best campsites requires a decent 4WD, complete with a confident driver.

For each free camp mentioned below, there's a three-day limit. You can take your dog but, as always, keep them under control. There are no facilities, so you'll need to be self-sufficient and take your rubbish out with you – including used toilet paper. Don't bury it or leave it in the bush. As always, check the tides before beach-driving. Call the Broome Visitor Centre on (08) 9195 2200 for current road conditions.

JAMES PRICE POINT (WALMADANY)

About 35km along Manari Road is the most well-known of the Northern Beaches' campsites, James Price Point.

In 2010, Western Australia's Premier Colin Barnett famously described James Price Point as an 'unremarkable' piece of coastline. Of course, there was an alternative agenda, with plans to build one of the world's largest gas hubs here. But environmental groups campaigned hard, and the development plans were eventually abandoned.

Due to the arrival of drones and Instagram, James Price Point is well known these days. But it's important to remember that this is a sacred place for local Indigenous people, who know it as Walmadan or Walmadany. To the Goolarabooloo people, Walmadany was a tribal man and a fierce protector of this coastline at the start of the 20th century. The Goolarabooloo believe that the spirits of Walmadany and his tribe are watching over it, and they caution visitors against venturing off and exploring this region alone.

QUANDONG (KARDILIKAN)

21km along Manari Road is the turn-off to Quandong. Here you'll find excellent fishing, whale watching and idyllic beachside camping. Known as Kardilakan to the Goolarabooloo people, this truly is a special place. The reef is home to corals and many sea creatures (look for turtles in the rockpools on the outgoing tide).

BARRED CREEK (NUWIRRAR)

14km along Manari Road is the Barred Creek turn-off (or alternatively, follow the track from Willie Creek). This is beach camping heaven with fishing, mud crabbing, and a turquoise tidal creek. Pick your campsite wisely – being close to the mangroves means sandflies. There are signs on the drive in with cultural information, directions and dangers to beware of (such as king brown snakes). At the T-section, turn right to head to the northern beaches or left to go south. Heed the tides and beware of the resident saltwater croc. 4WD is essential here. Stick to the tracks and keep out of the vegetation.

WILLIE CREEK (WIRRKINYMIRRI)

5km along Manari Road is the Willie Creek turn-off (or follow the track from Barred Creek). The pearl farm is popular with day trippers, but the creek is also loved by fishermen and 4WD explorers. There's great beach camping right on the sand. Though the water is pristine, beware, there are a couple of resident salties here.

01 Manari Road

02 Camping at James Price Point (Walmadany)

CAMP THE PENINSULA

The 220km stretch of coastline between Broome and Cape Leveque is beach camping heaven.

Ardi, which means northeast in the Bardi language, offers pristine coastlines, great fishing and unique cultural experiences with the local saltwater people. Camp on country at Indigenous-owned campgrounds and purchase your supplies from community stores. Read more at ardibeyondbroome.com.au.

BEAGLE BAY

Famous for its mother-of-pearl church, Beagle Bay also has some great places to camp, including Gnylmarung Retreat (gnylmarung.org.au) and Banana Well (bananawellgetaway.com.au). Gnylmarung offers basic beachside campsites for $20 per person, per night, with kids under 15 free and dogs allowed. Banana Well has unpowered camping for $50 per night for two adults. Add $20 for power. Dogs welcome. Read more on page 66.

MIDDLE LAGOON

A favourite spot for travellers since the 1990s, Middle Lagoon is owned and run by the Howard family. The campground has 70 unpowered campsites at $20 per person per night ($7 for kids 4-14 years) or $25 per person in the ridge campground, with great ocean views. middlelagoon.com.au. Read more on page 68. Alternatively, Mercedes Cove offers glamping and cabins from $180 per night. mercedescove.com.au.

LOMBADINA

There are some good camping options here. I recommend Djarindjin, as it's new and getting lots of great traveller reviews. It has sites from $50 per night for two adults, powered, or unpowered from $30. djarindjin.com.au. Lombadina's community on Thomas Bay also has a campground with unpowered bush campsites at $45 per night. lombadina.com. Alternatively, Chile Creek, about 7km south of Lombadina, offers some great beachside camping. (08) 9192 4141. Or, north, you've got Bullys Camp Djoodoon. Phone Geoff on (08) 9192 4359. Find out more on page 72.

PENDER BAY

Pender Bay Escape offers unpowered clifftop campsites for $20 per person per night, free for kids under 12. No dogs, no drones. Book via facebook.com/penderbayescape. Further around the bay, Smithy's Seaside Adventures offer powered and unpowered beachfront campsites from $24 per person per night and is dog friendly. Look up Smithy's Seaside Adventures-Embalgun on Facebook.

CYGNET BAY

Owned and run by third-generation pearl farmer, James Brown, and his family, Cygnet Bay is 200km north of Broome and is a working pearl farm. There are powered sites from $50 per night, and there's a great restaurant and pool 1km from the campsites. cygnetbaypearlfarm.com.au. Alternatively, next door is Gumbanan Bush Camp (read more on page 76).

BEAGLE BAY (NGARIUN BURR) 14/100 ☐

Visit the pearl shell church

Day trippers come for the pearl shell church. Travellers come for the opportunity to stay with locals nearby, fishing, crabbing, and sharing stories. All experience the heart and soul of this place.

At the unique Sacred Heart Church in Beagle Bay, 150km north of Broome, you'll feel like you've stepped inside the pearly gates. Because the Kimberley's tropical waters are abundant with pearl-producing oysters, Sacred Heart's interior has been elaborately decorated to create a mother-of-pearl mosaic. Adding to the distinctive vibe of this small church are Indigenous artworks by the local Bardi people. If you visit, drop some coins into the donation box.

The Nyul Nyul name is Ngariun Burr, meaning 'surrounded by springs'. It was given the name Beagle Bay in 1838 by Captain John Clements Wickham after his ship in which he surveyed the Kimberley coastline, the *HMS Beagle*. Self-governing since 1976, the Beagle Bay community has an interesting and, at times, sad history.

In 1918 during World War 1, Pallottine missionaries from Germany and the Sisters of St John of God from Ireland built the Sacred Heart church by hand, together with local Indigenous people. Before the missionaries' arrival, indigenous peoples had lived here for thousands of years. After the Aboriginal Act of 1905 enforced the removal of Indigenous children from their mothers, children were brought here from up to 1,000km away to be put under the state's care. Those kids are now grown up, and they run the community.

To visit the community, drop into the office upon arrival and pay the $5 fee. It's also worth grabbing a bite from the bakery (open each morning except for Saturdays). If you want to stay close by, Alphonse and

Delma Cox run the basic beachside camp of Gnylmarung Retreat. They grew up in Beagle Bay, married at the Sacred Heart Church and then moved to Gnylmarung in 1997, where they raised seven kids and started welcoming tourists in 2009. Turn off the Cape Leveque Road about 21km north of the Beagle Bay turn-off and follow the track until you see their sign (from the sealed road turn-off to Gnylmarung is about 30km, all up). Campsites are $20 per person per night, with kids under 15 free. Dogs allowed. gnylmarung.org.au

Alternatively, Banana Well (Burrguk) is another good option nearby, albeit very basic. There's a freshwater spring for drinking water, plus great fishing from Beagle Bay Creek. Like Zebedee Springs (page 107), the water here is known as fertility water, and many women who travel here have become pregnant. For bigger families or groups, Banana Well has a four-bedroom house (from $480 a night) and a three-bedroom house (from $390 a night). For smaller groups, there are one-bedroom cabins from $140 per night, plus powered camping ($70 per night for two adults) and unpowered camping ($50 per night for two adults). Dogs welcome. Bring insect spray. bananawellgetaway.com.au

MIDDLE LAGOON (WULGARDING) 15/100 ☐

Great fishing and coastal camping at this not-so-secret spot

Middle Lagoon was a favourite local getaway when we were kids, but word got out, and there's a steady crowd that returns year after year to soak in the goodness. And rightly so; it's beautiful.

In ancient mythology, the Dreamtime snake Wulgarding protected the area and gives it its traditional name. It's also called Midlagoon by locals in the nearby community of Beagle Bay. For the Howard family, it is home. It has been ever since Traci and the late Peter and Howard built Nature's Hideaway in 1991. They grew up in Beagle Bay and wanted to do more than be part of the welfare system. Securing the 99-year lease on this land allowed Peter to continue living and working on country while welcoming tourists to a piece of Australia that would otherwise be off-limits.

One of the main reasons that people return each year is for the great fishing. Catches include bluebone, coral trout, cod, mangrove Jack, or if you've brought a boat, Spanish mackerel, tuna and cobia further offshore. You can fish from the land or launch your tinny from the beach. There's also the seasonal migration of whales, mud crabbing in the creek, swimming in the shallow lagoon, snorkelling (BYO snorkels) and glorious sunsets into the ocean each day. Dogs are allowed (on lead), and Lagoon Beach is the dog beach.

The low-impact campground has 70 unpowered campsites at $20 per person per night ($7 for kids 4-14 years) or $25 per person in the ridge campground, which has great ocean views (in my opinion, worth paying a few more bucks for). If you have a big rig, let the Howards know when booking so they can allocate you a bigger site. Alternatively, there are cabins from $150 per night (shared ablutions with the

campground nearby), or $250 if you want a bigger cabin with its own ensuite. All of them have amazing sea views.

There are hot showers, a basic kiosk, bait and ice, a washing machine for guest use and patchy Wi-Fi. Mobile reception is also patchy here. It's best to bring all your supplies from Broome, including mozzie repellent and coils.

To get to Middle Lagoon, travel 21km past the Beagle Bay turn-off and then follow the corrugations for 33km to Middle Lagoon (let your tyre pressure down). Check availability and book at middlelagoon.com.au or phone 0499 085 086 with questions. Alternatively, the nearby Mercedes Cove offers a more exclusive glamping experience in its two eco tents and three cabins from $180 a night. facebook.com/mercedescove.

01 Red dirt roads are typical of the Dampier Peninsula. While the Cape Leveque Road is now sealed, many tracks to the camps still require a 4WD

PENDER BAY 16/100 ☐

Camp beside an ancient humpback whale nursery

Pender Bay has been known by only the most intrepid of travellers (and whale researchers) for years. But in 2019, images of rustic bathtubs on red cliffs began to circulate Instagram, and Pender was firmly cemented as a must-do spot for anyone driving north of Broome.

Located 190km from Broome (turn left towards Middle Lagoon off Cape Leveque Road, deflate your tyres and follow a rough 4WD track for about 30km), the true magic of Pender Bay is in its red-dirt-meets-sea scenery, set to a soundtrack of whales breathing nearby. Each July to October, the world's largest humpback whale migration passes along the Kimberley coastline, and Pender is a favourite spot for these goliaths to birth and rest. In 2006, Pender Bay was the site chosen to complete eight years of shore-based humpback whale surveys. Standing on top of the cliff, scientists and volunteers were surely bewildered at the sheer amount of whales passing by, with this great migration now numbering over 30,000 each season.

Nyul Nyul man Andrew Bowles, who helped to set up that scientific survey (initially funding it with his own money), and the Goojarr Goonyool Aboriginal Corporation have now opened a campground called Pender Bay Escape, welcoming a handful of visitors each season to its clifftop location. facebook.com/penderbayescape. Each site is unpowered, but you can light a campfire – you'll need it to cook the fish you've caught that day! There's a boat ramp if you've brought your tinny, or some great beach and bush walks if you haven't.

Demand for this campsite is high – booking months in advance is recommended (unless there's a last-minute cancellation), especially if you want the site with the bathtubs (site C2). Never mind if you can't get C2, every site is incredible, and you'll feel lucky to be one of the few who get the chance to stay here. Sites are just $20 per person per night, and kids under 12 are free. Day trippers are welcome for $10 a car, but dogs and drones aren't.

Further around the bay, Smithy's Seaside Adventures is run by a local Nyul Nyul family, who offer powered and unpowered beachfront campsites. There's 200m of beachfront access, great fishing, mud crabbing and whale watching. Smithy's is dog friendly and won't break the bank at $24 per person per night. Ph 0429 086 388.

01 Sisters Nicole and Kat Doyle enjoying sunset from campsite C2 at Pender Bay Escape

LOMBADINA AND DJARINDJIN

17/100 ☐

Woodfired bread and a bush church

Just before you hit the tip of the peninsula, about 190km up Cape Leveque Road, you'll find the two communities of Lombadina and Djarindjin. Lombadina has been open to tourists for years. I remember when my folks owned Broome Eco Adventures in Chinatown back in the 1990s, and Robert Sibasado, a respected Elder of the community, would drop in to talk about Lombadina.

The things that attract visitors to Lombadina include the beautiful old bush church, built in 1932, the art and craft centre (where you can buy traditionally carved pearl shells, trochus bangles and more), the bakery with its woodfired bread (available Monday, Wednesday, Friday) and the opportunity to experience Bardi country with its saltwater people. Fishing, mud crabbing and kayaking are a few activities on offer, or you can explore the beach at your own pace. Before exploring the area, check with the office which areas are open to visitors and which parts are only for the community. This is their land, and some areas are strictly off-limits.

Turning off Cape Leveque Road, you'll first encounter Djarindjin's roadhouse, with fuel and food. The community's great new campground has powered and unpowered sites from $30 per night for two adults, unpowered, or add $20 for power. djarindjin.com.au. Following the road toward the coast, you'll find Lombadina community on Thomas Bay. Check in with the office and pay the $10 fee for a day pass per car. Lombadina has self-contained cabins from $260 a night or budget rooms from $120 a night if you want to stay. There is also a campground, but I recommend staying at the newer campground at Djarindjin. Alternatively, the tiny community of Chile Creek, about 7km south of Lombadina, also offers some great beachside camping and fishing. Call ahead on (08) 9192 4141.

ONE ARM POINT (ARDYALOON) 18/100 ☐

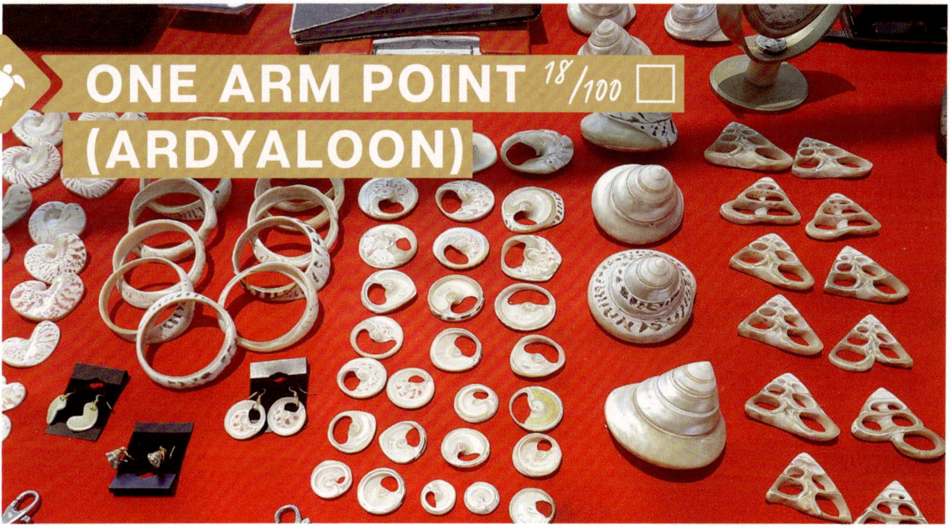

Visit the trochus shell hatchery

The northernmost settlement on the Dampier Peninsula, a 220km drive north of Broome, is One Arm Point, or Ardyaloon to the Bardi Jawa people.

Here, the landscape is dominated by red dirt and mangroves. These give way to white beaches and turquoise waters that the locals have no hesitation swimming in, despite the threat of crocs. Over at Jolongo Beach (south of town), schools of juvenile lemon sharks come in to feed off scraps. In the seagrass meadows further out, dugongs can often be seen.

The fishing is as good as it gets, thanks to the islands, bays and reefs carved over millennia by giant tides. Numerous ancient fish traps called myoorr in Bardi are scattered around the peninsula. When easterly trade winds blow (June to August), fish like mullet and trevally find shelter from the choppy water in these man-made traps before getting stuck at low tide. To this day, locals will venture to them and spear or collect the fish trapped against the stone walls laid thousands of years ago.

From April to November, visitors can join local rangers and marine biologists at the Ardyaloon Hatchery for a morning tour. The hatchery was set up for sustainable harvesting of trochus shells which were in decline due to overfishing. On the tour, you'll learn about local aquatic environments, marine life, and threats to both. Plenty of fish, coral and crustaceans are kept onsite.

Access to the community is $18 per adult and $5 for kids 6-16 years, including a guided hatchery tour and access to Middle Beach, Jologo Beach and Round Rock. Grab a visitor pass from the community office or the supermarket. The community requests that you don't drive around the housing area (ask for a map or see ardyaloonhatchery.com.au)

Nearby, the Daveys, a local Bardi family, run Gumbanan Bush Camp (gumbanan.com.au), which has unpowered sites for $20 per person per night or $10 for kids 11-16 and free under 10. Dogs are okay but tell them when you're booking. Pay upon arrival at Fish Trap Cafe (and grab a barra burger while you're there) if it's open. Otherwise, grab a site and slip into Bardi time – someone will see you eventually.

ARDI WITH THE BARDI 19/100 ☐

Explore the peninsula with a Bardi guide

The local Bardi (land) and Jawi (island) are saltwater people – they live by the tides and the seasons, with plentiful bush tucker in their backyard and fish and mud crabs in their front yard. To them, the Dampier Peninsula is known as Ardi. Amongst them are some fantastic local guides who are more than happy to show you around their traditional lands and tell stories of Dreamtime and life on the peninsula. These are genuinely enriching experiences, and I recommend that all visitors join at least one of the below tours or any of the many Indigenous tours offered privately at various campgrounds around the peninsula.

Brian Lee is one of the Kimberley's, actually Australia's, best guides and a real larrikin. I am always learning from him! With the gate to Kooljaman now locked, Brian takes guests down a backtrack as part of a tagalong tour, showing you his country while telling stories about traditional life on the peninsula. He'll fill your belly with bush tucker and mud crabs, always with a big smile on his dial. Meet at Djarindjin Roadhouse. See brianleetagalong.com.

Like Brian Lee, Bundy's Cultural Tours offers fantastic cultural tours on the tip of the peninsula, with bush tucker and bush medicine, a cook-up and stories. Book via djarindjin.com.au

Terry Hunter runs his trips from Cygnet Bay (Borrgoron) as he has a deep connection with this bay and its pearl farm – his family have lived and worked there for four generations. With his traditional knowledge of the land and sea, Terry shares pearling stories during his walking tours, or his Art Of Carving Riji tour teaches the art of riji shell carving. Book via coasttocreektours.com.au or at Cygnet Bay Pearl Farm's reception (see next page).

Bolo Angus comes from Ardyaloon (One Arm Point) and guides guests on walking tours of about four hours, sharing stories, songs and hunting methods while teaching about the six Bardi seasons. He offers a bush tucker and damper cook-up, too. Check out lullumbtours.com.au.

Rosanna Angus is a Jawi woman who runs Oolin Sunday Island Tours. Her family lived on Ewuny (Sunday Island), across the turbulent waters above the peninsula, during the Catholic mission days. Rosanna has plenty of stories to share during her island-hopping tour, starting at Cygnet Bay. Find out more at sundayislandtours.com.au.

01

01 Bardi Elder, Brian Lee, negotiating the best way to pick up this mud crab without being nipped

02 Terry Hunter leads a walking tour

02

CYGNET BAY 20/100 ☐ (BORRGORON)

A working pearl farm and waterfall reef

200km north of Broome, right up at the top of the peninsula, is Cygnet Bay (Borrgoron, in the Bardi name). I personally have a special connection with this spot, as my mate James Brown owns the pearl farm, and I proposed to my wife with a Cygnet Bay pearl. When it comes to precious gems, I don't think there's anything greater than something that has grown in the sea.

The Browns have owned and operated the farm for over 77 years after James' grandad sailed a wooden lugger through in 1946 and discovered that these waters were rich in Pinctada Maxima, the biggest of all pearl shells. Thus, the first Aussie-owned-and-run South Sea pearl farm was born. Through years of boom and bust in the pearling industry, it is one of WA's few remaining commercial pearl farms.

In 2009, the Brown family opened its pearl farm gates for visitors to dine, camp and glamp. James, a marine biologist, has also recently opened (and self-funded) the Kimberley Marine Research Station.

A visit to Cygnet Bay provides a unique look into life on a remote pearl farm. This is a spot that I visit with every safari tour group that I travel the peninsula with, and they all rave about it. There are some great tours

here, too, such as the Indigenous-operated tours on page 74, pearl shell carving, the Giant Tides boat tour and Waterfall Reef; a natural phenomenon where a reef emerges on outgoing tides to reveal a long and spectacular waterfall. Cygnet also has a few boats for hire, so if you have your recreational skipper's ticket, you can explore the coastline or go fishing on your own schedule.

Cygnet Bay is busiest from July to September. Visit during the shoulder months to get this gem all to yourself! Book ahead for tours to Waterfall Reef and other experiences as they depend on the tide. Visit cygnetbaypearlfarm.com.au or phone (08) 9192 4283. If you can't get to Cygnet Bay, the farm has a boutique store on Dampier Terrace in Chinatown. I recommend buying some pearl meat from their showroom and cooking it up.

01 Waterfall Reef on an outgoing tide

02 Glamping tents at Cygnet Bay

03 Marine biologist and third generation pearl farmer, James Brown

DERBY & THE GIBB RIVER ROAD

Outback road trips don't get more fun than the legendary Gibb River Road. The 660km old cattle route is now one of Australia's most iconic 4WD trails with gorges, waterfalls and clear, starry nights. But, despite it becoming more well-known these days, it still retains its raw and undeveloped appeal.

It's awesome to think that before the Gibb River Road's reconstruction, cattle used to be walked from the Kimberley's remote cattle stations to either Derby or Wyndham. What a mission! In the 1950s, the Commonwealth upgraded the road to make transportation by vehicle an easier option. However, 'easier' is subjective. It's easier to 4WD across it than it is to drove cattle, but it's still a rough road, so pack spare tyres and a repair kit, and then prepare your body for corrugations.

While a 4WD is highly recommended, I'll never forget meeting two blokes, Jono and Leroy, who took on the mighty Gibb in their 1967 VW Beetle! For this mission, they went later in the season (around September, if I remember correctly) when the Pentecost River crossing had been reduced to puddles. Earlier in the Dry Season, the Pentecost can be a raging torrent that is simply uncrossable. Usually, the river drops enough to open the road from May to October, but it's not uncommon for it to be closed until mid-May after big Wet Season rains.

Nick 'Honey Badger' Cummins, comes face-to-face with Moo, a friendly bull at Home Valley Station

While the region surrounding the road is still heavily influenced by pastoralism, this is slowly changing. In recent times, the return of El Questro to its Traditional Owners has seen the end of a pastoral lease first granted by the Crown in 1903. Another spot devoid of cattle is the 300,000-hectare Mornington Wildlife Sanctuary (page 92), whose tourism operations exist to fund its wildlife conservation efforts. On the flip side, Home Valley Station, under the management of Balanggarra Traditional Custodians, is a working cattle station with a fantastic Indigenous hospitality training program. They have a breeding program for Brahman cattle, and one of their most famous and friendly residents is a large bull named Moo.

On the subject of change, a few locations along the Gibb River Road have recently been renamed. The Wunaamin-Miliwundi Ranges is one example. This dominant mountain range in the western Gibb River Road was previously named the King Leopold Ranges in 1879 in honour of a Belgian monarch who never visited the Kimberley and was known for committing genocide in the Congo. Wunaamin-Miliwundi combines the Bunuba and Ngarinyin traditional names for those ranges. Other places that have been renamed in recent times include Dalmanyi (Bell Gorge) and Dimalurru (Tunnel Creek). I'm sure that we can expect more changes to come.

No matter what your expectations are, you'll be blown away by the beauty of this part of Australia. There's so much to discover, from magical waterfalls and swimming holes to incredible stargazing and a rich cultural history to learn about. While there are a few general stores, fuel stops and homestead restaurants along the way, it's important to remember that the Gibb is remote and seasonal, so services come at a premium. This is a place to enjoy one day at a time. If you're following an itinerary, I suggest you keep it loose to allow longer stays in places you love. This will also give you time to sit and chat with some of the station's managers or long-time residents, who often have some great stories to tell. Or simply sit and watch the wildlife and landscape go about its daily business in this timeless part of Australia.

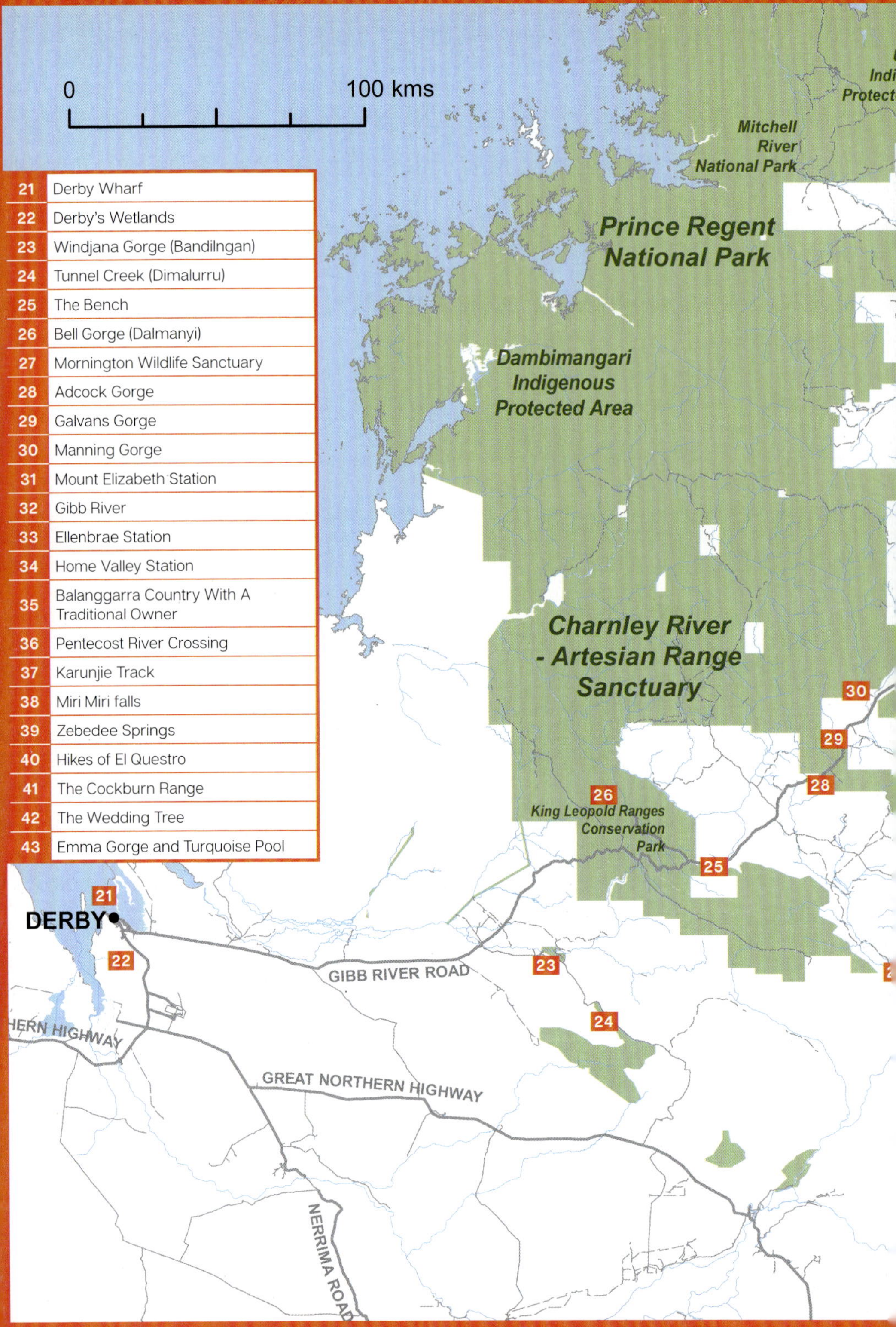
0
100 kms
21 Derby Wharf
22 Derby's Wetlands
23 Windjana Gorge (Bandilngan)
24 Tunnel Creek (Dimalurru)
25 The Bench
26 Bell Gorge (Dalmanyi)
27 Mornington Wildlife Sanctuary
28 Adcock Gorge
29 Galvans Gorge
30 Manning Gorge
31 Mount Elizabeth Station
32 Gibb River
33 Ellenbrae Station
34 Home Valley Station
35 Balanggarra Country With A Traditional Owner
36 Pentecost River Crossing
37 Karunjie Track
38 Miri Miri falls
39 Zebedee Springs
40 Hikes of El Questro
41 The Cockburn Range
42 The Wedding Tree
43 Emma Gorge and Turquoise Pool
Mitchell River National Park
Prince Regent National Park
Dambimangari Indigenous Protected Area
Charnley River - Artesian Range Sanctuary
King Leopold Ranges Conservation Park
DERBY
GIBB RIVER ROAD
GREAT NORTHERN HIGHWAY
NERRIMA ROAD
21
22
23
24
25
26
28
29
30

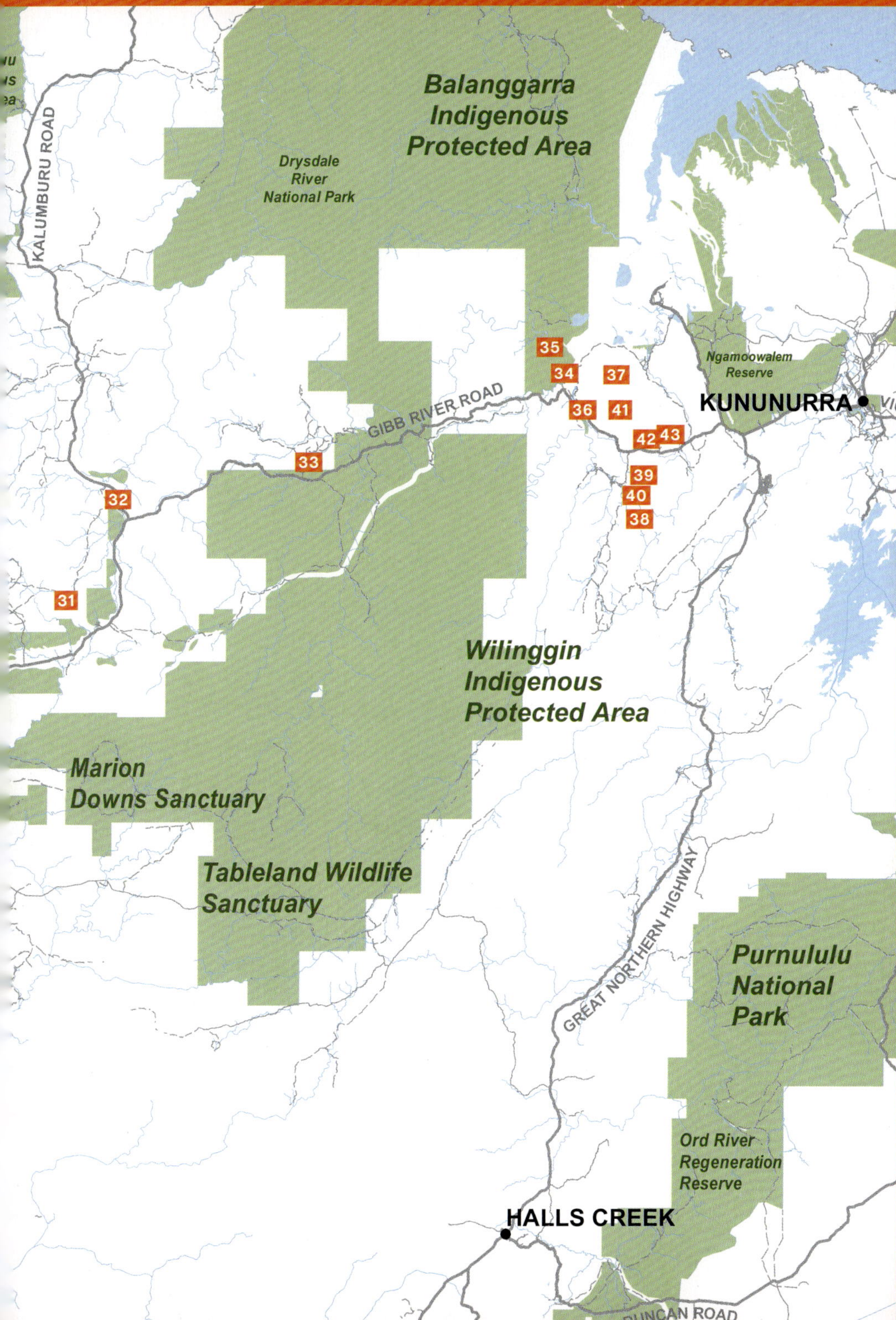
Balanggarra Indigenous Protected Area
Drysdale River National Park
KALUMBURU ROAD
GIBB RIVER ROAD
Ngamoowalem Reserve
KUNUNURRA
31
32
33
34
35
36
37
38
39
40
41
42
43
Wilinggin Indigenous Protected Area
Marion Downs Sanctuary
Tableland Wildlife Sanctuary
GREAT NORTHERN HIGHWAY
Purnululu National Park
Ord River Regeneration Reserve
HALLS CREEK
DUNCAN ROAD

DERBY WHARF 21/100 ☐

Watch the world's largest tropical tide rushing in from King Sound

Fringed by the tidal mudflats on the edge of King Sound, Derby, 200km northeast of Broome, serves as the western gateway to the Gibb River Road. Derby is famous for having the highest tidal range of any Australian port. Watching the tide from the wharf as it floods in during spring and king tides is remarkable.

The original wharf was built in 1894, and a horse-drawn tramway connected it to the town. The current wharf is over 55 years old and is the best spot to catch a magnificent sunset over the sound. Bring your fishing gear and throw a line for a golden grunter or blue salmon, or set a pot to lure a big, fat mud crab! If you're looking for a fishing guide, chat with Katlyn Yeeda at the Derby Visitor Centre. Known locally as the Derby Jetty Queen, she was given the honorary title after she reeled in a 110cm black jewfish (mulloway) on a handline. Katlyn loves sharing tips with visitors, and she may even take you on a fishing tour herself if she has a day off.

Derby is also the closest town to the iconic Horizontal Falls. You can join a local cruise operator from Derby and head out into King Sound and the nearby Buccaneer Archipelago (and Horizontal Falls). There are also scenic flights to the falls, including the option to land on the water in a seaplane and then stay overnight on a floating pontoon close to the falls. Ask the Derby Visitor Centre for availability; visit derbytourism.com.au or call (08) 9191 1426.

DERBY'S WETLANDS

22/100 ☐

Important wetlands that are home to over 200 bird species

While Derby isn't well-known amongst birdwatchers, over 200 species have been recorded in and around the town. Funnily enough, one of the first spots that local twitchers suggest is the sewerage ponds (a.k.a. Derby Wetland and Bird Observatory). Although visiting the 'poo ponds' doesn't sound very enticing, this wetland just south of town (accessible from the end of Conway Street) is one of the best spots to look for water birds such as waders and ducks. Here, a controlled amount of wastewater is released from the treatment plant, creating an important wetland area for birds. There's an observation hut where you can chill in the shade while you look for birds, such as the sacred kingfisher or the Pacific blue duck.

If hanging out near wastewater plants doesn't sound like your cup of tea, head to the 3km looped Joonjoo Botanical Trail off Worsley Road (about 5km south of Derby). This trail is excellent for bush birds, and the Derby Visitor Centre has a great trail guide and map. In addition, the track has some great signs with information about the Nyinkina peoples and the bushtucker and medicines found in this region.

Beyond town and just 15km south of the Prison Boab Tree is the turn-off into the Munkajarra Wetland. Here, you might see larger birds like brolga or jabiru (the black-necked stork) or smaller beauties, including red-backed fairywrens. To find this spot, navigate about 20km south of Derby until you see a sign for the wetland on the side of the highway. Turn down a 4WD track and navigate through the bush, opening and closing two gates behind you while looking for birds as you make your way in. The condition of the track will depend on how recently a grader has been through after the latest Wet Season rains.

WINDJANA GORGE (BANDILNGAN) 23/100 ☐

If you want to see crocs in the wild, this is the spot

Located 150km east of Derby, Bandilngan (Windjana Gorge) National Park stretches for 3.5km, its limestone walls towering 100m above you. Walk along the edge of the Lennard River, following the Time Walk Trail to spot fossils embedded into the limestone walls, then step out onto a beach crowded with freshwater crocodiles basking in the sunshine.

The Lennard River reduces to small pools in the Dry Season and is one of the best places to view freshies. Although they're not considered dangerous to humans, giving them some space is wise.

Windjana Gorge is known by the Indigenous name Bandilngan. It has great cultural significance to the local Bunuba people, who believe that the Wandjina creation spirits reside here. You can learn more about the area with a local indigenous guide; I recommend Dillon Andrews of Bungoolee Tours. bungoolee.com.au.

If you're staying at the campground, get up early to enjoy a riverside walk at dawn and then return to photograph the rock in the glowing afternoon sun. Within the national park, you can also visit the limestone ruins of Lillimilura Police Station; a historical homestead turned police outpost constructed in 1884, which is located 2km away from Windjana Gorge.

TUNNEL CREEK (DIMALURRU) 24/100 ☐

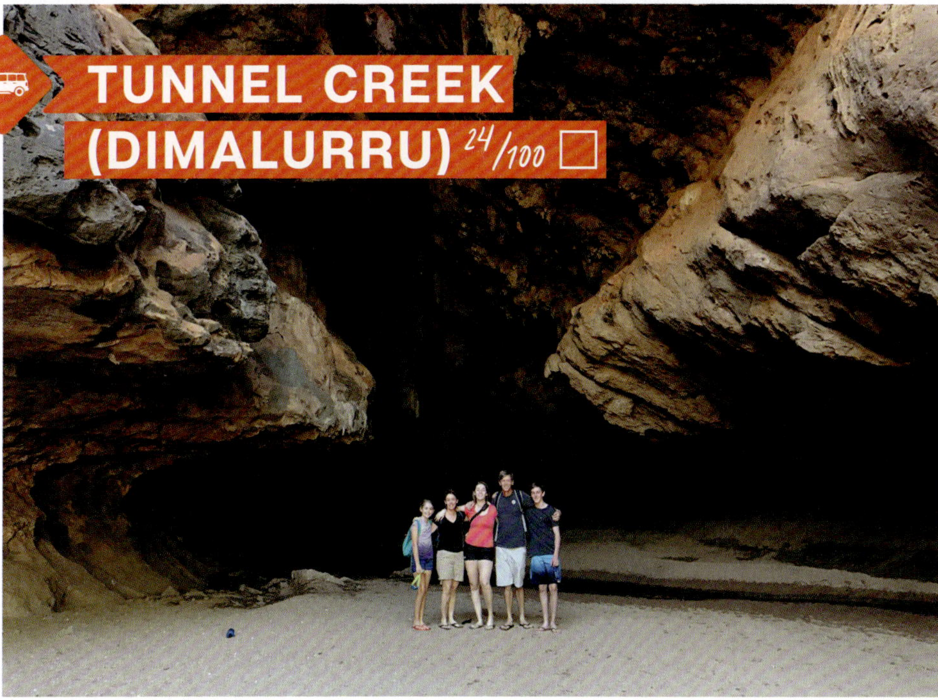

Wade through the cave by torchlight

What brings travellers to Tunnel Creek National Park is an eerily dark cave tunnelled into the Napier Range and the wet walk through it, spotlighting the little flying foxes that cling restlessly to stalactites overhead. Wade through the sometimes knee-deep water for 750m (keep an eye out for the glowing eyes of the resident freshwater crocs) to discover a billabong on the other side. It's not the most leisurely walk, so expect to do some scrambling. Aim to arrive earlier in the morning to avoid the tour groups unless you are in a group with local operator Bungoolee Tours, which offer genuine, local insight into the tunnel's significance and history.

Tunnel Creek is significant to Traditional Custodians, the Bunaba people, who know it as Dimalurru. It was the hideout for Jandamarra, a freedom fighter known as 'Pidgeon' who became an outlaw after Indigenous people were forced off their tribal lands and onto pastoral stations to work. Jandamarra was shot dead at the entrance to Tunnel Creek by the Aboriginal tracker, Micki, who was working with the police.

You can get to it either from the Great Northern Highway or the Gibb River Road by turning onto Fairfield-Leopold Downs Road (which connects through from the Gibb to the highway). Although Tunnel Creek is much easier to access from the highway and is about 90km from Fitzroy Crossing, it's a more adventurous trip from the Gibb. The road will probably be impassable after rain. There's no camping at Tunnel Creek, but the campsite at Windjana Gorge isn't too far away.

THE BENCH 25/100 ☐

The prettiest sunrise spot in the western Kimberley

After writing the first edition of this guidebook, some people asked if there are any special spots along the Gibb where I take my guests for sunrise or sunset. I immediately thought of The Bench (the Wedding Tree on page 111 is another spot). I believe this is one of the Kimberley's best places to watch the sunrise.

There's no tourist sign saying 'The Bench'; this is just the name that I and other local guides know it as. On almost every Gibb trip, whether I'm with guests, friends, or family, I come here, and it never disappoints. Because it's also only a 15-minute drive west from Imintji Campground, it's easy to get to and always worth the pre-dawn start (you don't watch the sunset here, as it's behind the ranges to the west). Sometimes other people are here, and we all have a yarn while we watch the sun colour the hills in classic Dry Season, twilight hues. Other times, our group will have it all to ourselves. Either way, it's magic.

Coming from Imintji Campground, travel 13km west along the Gibb River Road and turn into the carpark (on Google Maps, the coordinates are 17°10'00.0" S 125°20'51.9" E). At The Bench (take note, there is no actual bench, so BYO camp chair), you'll be looking out onto the eastern side of the Wunaamin-Miliwundi Ranges, the Precipice Ranges and the Isdell Range to the left. Isdell Range is home to Bell Gorge (Dalmanyi) and Isdell Gorge, where various ancient Indigenous art (specifically Wandjina art) can be found. Isdell was named in 1898 by the pastoralist and explorer Frank Hann, who navigated through these ranges and marked out the central Kimberley region for cattle grazing.

STAY

Throughout this chapter, I mention various gorges, waterfalls and stations, and within those listings, I've included information on nearby campsites.

On this page, I'm shining a spotlight on Indigenous-owned stays along with Gibb. Right now, there aren't many. But with your support, perhaps we'll see more communities opening up to travellers, which will provide Indigenous people with income, employment and the chance to showcase their culture.

GIBB RIVER STATION

Named after the small wallabies seen here, the Goondalee Campsite at Gibb River Station advertises itself as the best value in the Kimberley, with camping at the price of $30 per vehicle per night. The campsite has hot showers and a grassy lawn, and it's conveniently adjacent to the store and homestead, next to a big mango tree. Owned by the Ngallagunda Aboriginal Corporation, the property is a working cattle station with a homestead, community store, fuel, and an Aboriginal Art Centre. Visit gibbriverstation.com.au or phone (08) 9191 7494.

IMINTJI

Camping With Custodians is an Australian-first initiative promoting campgrounds on Indigenous lands which are operated by their communities. One of the first to jump on board with this initiative was the Iminjti community, just 8km east of the turn-off to Dalmanyi (Bell Gorge). The Imintji (Ngarinyin) people provide a shady, grassed central area, hot showers and a camp kitchen. Their store sells diesel, basic groceries, coffee and art. Unpowered campsites are $19 per adult, $15 for kids (5-15 years) or free for kids under 5. Visit imintji.com.au.

HOME VALLEY STATION

Home Valley is a working cattle station and an Indigenous hospitality training centre. There's a fantastic bar area – Dusty's Bar and Grill – plus a range of accommodation, from fancy Grass Castle cabins overlooking Bindoola Creek to two dog-friendly campsites. The Homestead Camp offers powered and unpowered sites, hot showers, and close access to Dusty's Bar and the swimming pool. Otherwise, the bush camp is 4km away (next to the Pentecost River) and has unpowered sites and hot showers. Visit home-valley.com.au.

BELL GORGE 26/100 ☐ (DALMANYI)

A stunning gorge with a cascading waterfall and great camping nearby

It's the jewel of the Gibb, a gem of a spot in the Wunaamin Miliwundi Ranges (formerly known as the King Leopold Ranges from 1879 to 2020). Located about 238km from Derby, Bell Gorge is a favourite for many travellers, and it's easy to see why this is one of the Kimberley's most popular waterholes.

After walking 750m from the carpark along a rocky track, you'll arrive at this magic spot. At the top of the waterfall, you can look over the edge to where Bell Creek cascades 50m down from the top creek over sandstone rocks, filling the huge swimming hole below. Swimming in the top creek is great if you don't feel like scrambling to the bottom pool. The view is grand from up here! The bottom pool, below the cascade, is where most tourists stop for a swim before walking back up to the top creek and returning to their car or the nearby Dulundi (Silent Grove) campground. Bring a floaty and some tucker, and you'll easily spend the day here relaxing and floating. Prepare for crowds, though, in the main swimming hole. Just about every tour group and private vehicle travelling the Gibb stops here.

01 Walk across Bell Creek and then follow the trail down into the waterhole below

02 Follow the water to find the bottom pool, which you'll likely have to yourself

I recommend getting out of bed and onto the trail early while the tour groups eat their breakfast. Once the crowd arrives, follow the water on its northwest journey toward the Isdell River. You'll discover many gorgeous swimming spots and probably have them to yourself.

If you're planning on spending the day here, the best places to camp nearby are Dulundi (Silent Grove) campground, which has unpowered sites, toilets and solar showers, or at Imintji Community. In the Ngarinyin language, Imintji means a place to sit down. Read more on page 89.

MORNINGTON WILDLIFE SANCTUARY 27/100 ☐

Canoe through the walls of Dimond Gorge or spot for a rare Gouldian finch

At 88km off the Gibb River Road, Mornington Wildlife Sanctuary demands some dedication to access, but those who make the mission are richly rewarded. Your two-hour detour ends with great camping, bushwalking, and sweet swimming spots. This is a place to pull up for a few days, or a week, to thoroughly explore the terrain.

Turning off the Gibb at Mount House Station, you'll find a radio booth to call ahead to check with staff about campsite availability and current road conditions. From there, about 1.5 to 2 hours of quintessential Kimberley scenery will have you anticipating what's around the next bend. And it only gets better as you get further along.

At the end of the road, you'll find Mornington Wilderness Camp, owned and managed by the non-profit Australian Wildlife Conservancy. The Conservancy does a brilliant job of managing the $3,000km^2$ wildlife sanctuary. It provides fantastic overviews of the local flora and fauna to travellers through slide nights and guided nature walks (book one on arrival).

Take a walk around Little Annie Creek, especially early in the morning or late in the afternoon, to look for flighty finches and other birds.

As a wildlife sanctuary, it has strict rules around domestic animals (sorry, no dogs here), drones (leave it in your car), fishing (again, leave your gear in the car) and campfires (none here). There are unpowered campsites by the creek with plenty of shade, plus toilets and hot showers close by. There are also African-style safari tents overlooking Annie Creek, usually chockers with tour groups that travel in on big 4WD buses.

The Bush Bar and restaurant is an excellent spot to stand around and have a yarn at night, though the campground has good BBQ facilities if you'd prefer to save your silvers and cook your own food. Should you find yourself at the bar chatting to a driver of one of those big tour buses, ask them for their schedule for the following day, so you can plan to be elsewhere when their tour group overtakes those spots.

The best places to visit are Blue Bush Billabong, Sir John Gorge and Dimond Gorge. These spots are nice for swimming and canoes can be rented from the camp. With its towering gorge walls and lack of crowds, Dimond Gorge is one of my favourites in the Kimberley, and the best way to experience it is with a paddle in your hand. It's a leisurely 2km trip through the gorge, so pack a picnic and a dry bag.

Keep your eyes open, and bring your binoculars. The wildlife sanctuary is home to over 208 recorded bird species, including purple-crowned fairywrens and the rare Gouldian finch. If you're lucky, you may also spot a short-eared rock wallaby and some freshwater crocs as you paddle down the gorge. Visit australianwildlife.org or email mornington@australianwildlife.org. Visitor permits are $25 per vehicle.

ADCOCK GORGE 28/100 ☐

A freshwater gorge with fewer people

Despite being close to the Gibb, Adcock is one of the quieter gorges, but it's no less beautiful than the more popular ones like Bell Gorge. Located on Mount House Station (owned by Australian media mogul Kerry Stokes, who also has a mansion behind the dunes at Cable Beach), this freshwater gorge is 5km off the Gibb via a rocky 4WD track.

You're likely to find yourself alone in this beautiful gorge at any given time. After driving down the bumpy road, you'll arrive at a short track that leads past a waterlily pond and into the swimming hole. If you dare, rocky ledges provide platforms for jumping into the deep green water below (of course, always check the depth first). You can walk around the side of the gorge to shower underneath the trickling waterfall or sit and soak up the tranquillity of this peaceful spot. There's also rock art on Adcock's cliff face, over to the left-hand side and scattered throughout.

There is no camping in this area; the closest is at Mount Barnett (Manning Gorge). Mount House Station's staff and Gibb River Road rangers keep an eye on the area, as it's been left a mess before, which nearly led to it being shut for good. So please keep it tidy, and if anyone has dropped any rubbish, please pick it up and take it with you so the next person can enjoy the gorge, too.

GALVANS GORGE 29/100 ☐

The closest swimming hole and rock art site to the Gibb

A cruisey 750m stroll from the carpark on the edge of the Gibb River Road, this oasis in the Phillips Range is one not to be missed. Here you'll find a beautiful pool for a refreshing swim at the bottom of a waterfall (which slows down as the Dry Season progresses) and a boab tree standing proudly above, completing a quintessential Kimberley scene.

Check out the rock art on the wall behind the tree swing (but never touch or interfere with the paintings) and enjoy spotting the water monitors warming up in the sun on the rocks. Unfortunately, there are fewer of them around now, as their population has sadly declined since cane toads reached the Kimberley.

As the Gibb's most accessible gorge, Galvans is (not surprisingly) visited by just about everyone driving this old stock route. If it's too busy here, head across to Adcock Gorge, which you'll likely have to yourself. The two gorges are so close you can just come back to Galvans later when it's quieter.

MANNING GORGE 30/100 ☐

A waterfall cascading into a deep pool halfway along the Gibb

A firm favourite along the Gibb River Road, Manning has it all. Riverside camping? Tick. General store with supplies at the entrance? Waterfall to spend the day at? Tick.

Upon arriving at Barnett River Roadhouse, pay the entrance fee and proceed 7km north to the riverside camping area. The 5.6km return gorge walk begins on the other side of the river. Unlike the old days when you had to swim across, there's now a little boat with a rope to ferry you to the other side.

Being less shady (and more exposed) than many other walks along the Gibb, the 1 to 1.5-hour walk into the swimming hole can get hot, so avoid the midday sun if you can. There's some rock clambering in places, particularly close to the end, so wear shoes with decent tread and ankle support. The track is well marked, and it's a scenic walk, despite the lack of shade making it hard going in some parts. When you get to the end of the track, keep an eye out for the rock art on the right-hand wall (once you clearly sight the waterfall for the first time). The beautiful, deep gorge at the trail's end is worth the walk, especially after some rain when the falls are at their best. Not up for the trek? No worries; the river at the campground is a beaut spot to take a dip, too.

You can choose between two campsites nearby if you want to spend the day here. Either the riverside camping at the beginning of the gorge trail or at Mount Barnett Roadhouse, which has bathroom facilities. The Roadhouse, which is also the Kupungarri community store, is a good spot to stock up on some fruit and vegetables or supplies for fishing. This store can get very busy during the peak season as it's the primary fuel and supply store for the Gibb River Road, so be patient or get in early to fuel up. Also, do not move your vehicle before paying, regardless of how many cars are stacked up behind you; an alarm sounds inside the store, and you'll get a frown from the friendly staff inside for not reading their signs.

01 Pulling back the little boat that ferries hikers across to the start of the trail

MOUNT ELIZABETH STATION 31/100 □

A working cattle station with a real classic Kimberley feel

Mount Elizabeth Station Stay is a half-million-acre, fully-operational cattle station. The homestead is a top spot to base yourself for a night or so, with great camping, accommodation and food.

Just 19km from the station's homestead is a white sandy beach and a lovely gorge called Warla Gorge (also known as the Hann River Gorge). This is an excellent spot to swim or chill out underneath the shady trees. There's a fee of $20 per vehicle (or $15 if you're staying overnight at Mount Elizabeth), which includes access to all the gorges and walking trails on the property.

About 8km south of the Mount Elizabeth homestead, via a challenging, high clearance 4WD track that will test you and your vehicle, you'll find another lovely gorge called Wunnamurra. There's a permanent swimming hole, Indigenous rock art, and white sandy beaches under the falls. Few crew know about this gorge, yet it's one of the best along the Gibb. The best time to visit is early morning or late afternoon to avoid the midday sun. The falls are best early in the Dry Season after getting topped up by rain.

If you have heard of the Munja Track and were hoping to get there (accessible from Mount Elizabeth), unfortunately, it's closed to all vehicles for the time being.

Cross the Gibb River, but not on the Gibb River Road

On every tour down the Gibb, I always take the turn-off up Kalumburu Road to this spot just 5km north of the Gibb River Road. The headwaters of the Gibb River begin at the Caroline and Gibb Ranges, running in a northerly direction to eventually merge with the Drysdale River (one of its tributaries). It crosses Kalumburu Road (not the actual Gibb River Road) and makes for a nice stop to grab a bite to eat while you watch for finches, egrets, herons, rainbow bee-eaters and, of course, freshwater crocs. I've seen plenty of decent-sized freshies here, baking on the rocks under the hot midday sun.

The surveyor Charles Crossland named the river in 1901 after the geologist Andrew Gibb Maitland, who was on the expedition when Crossland first recorded seeing the river. The cattle route then took on Gibb's name, too. The Ngarinyin (pronounced Na-rin-gin) people are the Traditional Owners of this country. Therefore, permission to leave the road for any reason beyond the small parking bay should be obtained from Clyde at Gibb River Station (page 89).

Beyond this point and venturing further north, you'll see the landscape begin to change quite dramatically. Gibb River has a distinct feel to it, and if you sit down for a cuppa and soak it all in, you'll sense that this truly is the land that time forgot.

ELLENBRAE STATION 33/100 ☐

Fresh scones and mango frappes

Outback hospitality doesn't get any better, and nothing says 'outback hospitality' like fresh scones with jam and cream! Out on the Gibb, a sign grabs the attention of passers-by, directing them into the land of the scone – something to look forward to after hours of bumping through the dusty outback. The scones also taste great when accompanied by Ellenbrae's delicious mango frappes.

Located 230km from Kununurra, this almost million-acre station (owned since 2005 by the Grollo family from Melbourne) has more than scones and a good feed. For overnight guests, there are two beaut billabongs for swimming, plus a choice between campsites and rustic cabins. There are also unique, wood-fired (donkey) showers to wash off the dust.

You could relax for hours on the verandah, watching tiny double-barred and crimson finches flitting about the gardens and nibbling at feeders hanging around the deck. There's genuine outback hospitality on offer, and Ellebrae is conveniently located just 5km off the Gibb. Visit ellenbraestation.com.au.

HOME VALLEY STATION 34/100 ☐

Indigenous hospitality on a working cattle station on the Gibb

Head 114km west of Kununurra along the Gibb River Road, and you'll find yourself at Home Valley Station (whose brand reads HV8). The experience begins as soon as you arrive at what is possibly the coolest gate in the Kimberley, inscribed with the words from an Aboriginal proverb that says, "We are all visitors to this time, this place. We are just passing through. Our purpose here is to observe, to learn, to grow... and then we return home." Interestingly, Queen Elizabeth II also used this quote in a 2011 speech she made while visiting Perth.

In 1999, HV8 was purchased by the Indigenous Land Corporation on behalf of the Balanggarra people of the east Kimberley. Today, HV8 is a working cattle station, an Indigenous training facility and one of the highlights of the Gibb River Road. While it shares a border with El Questro Station (the border is the Pentecost River), the vibe of the two properties is very different.

Some of my favourite things to do here include fishing, horseriding, chilling out around the campfire and eating at Dusty Bar and Grill. Bindoola Gorge is well worth a visit, with its 90-foot walls, rockpools and birdlife. Travelling approximately 15km from Home Valley's homestead, you will arrive at a blink-and-you'll-miss-it sign that directs you to a carpark. Follow the 3km return walking trail to arrive at the deep green gorge. If you visit early in the season and there's been recent rain, then you'll also see Bindoola Falls falling. But at any time of year, you'll be smitten by the beauty of this sandstone gorge. See home-valley.com.au.

BALANGGARRA COUNTRY WITH A TRADITIONAL OWNER 35/100 ☐

One of the most enriching cultural experiences you can have in the Kimberley is to go fishing with a Traditional Owner

In Balanggarra country, at the eastern end of the Gibb River Road, you can do this with Sam Birch, known locally as Birchy.

The Balanggarra Indigenous Protected Area is over one million hectares (almost half the size of Tasmania), covering land and sea in the eastern Kimberley. The northern portion is called blue water country, and it includes the King George River, Cape Londonderry and some offshore reefs and islands. The south is called brown water country, and it's made up of the Cambridge Gulf (page 170) and the region north of the Gibb River Road around the Cockburn Range, including Home Valley Station (previous page).

This region was handed back to the Balanggarra people in 2013 after nearly 20 years of fighting for native title recognition. With self-governance of their land, the Balanggarra Aboriginal Corporation together with the Balanggarra Rangers, can care for country in their own way. They can combine their traditional knowledge with modern scientific methods while simultaneously looking after sites of great cultural

significance. They can also share tourism experiences on their own terms, allowing for more Indigenous experiences and the employment of Indigenous people.

For Balanggarra man Sam Birch, tourism allows him to showcase the country and tell stories and share his traditional knowledge of bush foods and bush medicines. But what he loves the most is fishing and hunting. Birchy runs some fantastic full-day tours for $450 per person ($250 for kids), where you'll have a chance to fish for barra and other species (depending on the time of year). He also runs a full-day fishing and bush turkey hunting trip, including a Welcome To Country smoking ceremony for $700 per person ($360 for kids). Ask him about his extended 4WD tours if you're after something longer. Check out facebook.com/birchysfishingtours (where you can also read reviews) or give him a buzz on 0459 540 763.

01 Barramundi for days

02 Bush turkey

03 Birchy 'The Barra King' strikes again

PENTECOST RIVER CROSSING 36/100 ☐

An iconic river crossing and photographers' favourite

The Pentecost River crossing is one of the most iconic images of the Gibb River and the Kimberley. While it's best at sunset when the Cockburn Ranges are glowing orange, you can come here at any time of the day and find people admiring it as cars drive across the river.

The crossing is 120km from Kununurra down the Gibb River Road and, being so close to the town, is a popular spot for locals to come fishing for barramundi. There's plenty of wildlife to spot here, and, on any given day, you might see dingoes, red or yellow-tailed black cockatoos, and even estuarine (saltwater) crocodiles (no swimming here). Be careful if you cast a line for barra and stand well back from the water's edge.

While the river crossing and the presence of salties might be intimidating, it's actually a reasonably straightforward crossing once the water level has dropped after the Wet Season rains. Early in the Dry Season, around April or May, the Pentecost River can be deep, swift flowing and challenging to cross. As the months pass, the crossing gets easier. The hard, rocky bottom provides a solid, albeit bumpy ride.

This river is the natural border that splits El Questro and Home Valley stations. They are two of the most popular spots to visit in the east Kimberley, so the Main Roads crew recently upgraded the road to blacktop (bitumen) from Kununurra to the eastern side of the crossing. Once you're across, it's dirt from there on, apart from the jump-ups (or hills), which have been sealed to assist the cattle trucks and to stop the hills from getting washed away each Wet Season.

KARUNJIE TRACK 37/100 ☐

An outback track for serious off-roaders

Corrugations, creek crossings, floodplains, wash-outs and cattle: this old stock route is not for the faint-hearted, but the views of the western side of the Cockburn Range sure are glorious!

The adventure starts at the Gibb River Road's Pentecost River crossing. Once you get to the eastern banks of the Pentecost, turn north and follow the track along the river before it eventually swings east through Balanggarra country in the northern half of El Questro. It eventually reaches King River Road near Diggers Rest Station and the Prison Boab Tree. The 86km track takes most of the day to complete as long as the road isn't boggy from rain (June to October is best). Bring your fishing gear to catch barra from the banks of the Pentecost, but beware, this is saltwater crocodile territory!

There's great camping at Diggers Rest Station, a 20,000-acre working cattle station on the Cockburn Range's northern side, owned by Roderick (a third-generation Kimberley local) and Alida Woodland. Diggers is known for its great camping and amazing horseriding treks, from two hours to one week in length. diggersreststation.com.au

To help keep the cattle in, close each gate you open as you travel the Karunjie. But beware; occasionally, some of the gates have been locked (cattle have suspiciously gone missing from Roderick's mob). The station might also lock some gates temporarily when mustering is on, so be prepared to double back if this is the case.

MIRI MIRI FALLS 38/100 ☐

A spring-fed waterfall that you'll have all to yourself

There are a few reasons why Miri Miri is one of my favourite waterfalls in the Kimberley, and the fact that my beautiful daughter shares the name is one of those reasons! This waterhole is found within a remote part of El Questro. There are no roads here, so few folks know about it and even fewer get to enjoy it. The waters emerge from a spring a few kilometres back in the hill and feed into Moonshine Creek, which eventually runs into the Pentecost River.

I've done some terrific extended hikes around this area over the years, and it's some of the most stunning terrain in the world, in my opinion. There are sandstone ridges and cliffs, turquoise waters in places, pools lined with palm trees and ferns, and waterholes full of fish. You'll always be left wanting more. But as time always seems to be of the essence in this modern world, the only public access nowadays is on a two-hour helicopter tour. This flight is about 15 minutes each way, and you'll get about an 1.5 hours to picnic and swim under the falls.

If arriving by chopper is special, having this waterfall and swimming hole all to yourself is a real treat; think palm trees, rainbows and an ancient landscape that'll take your dreaming to the next level. This spring-fed waterfall cascades 50m into the pool below, surrounded by Livistona palms and paperbark trees. The chopper flight offers a bird's-eye view over valleys, gorges and an endless savannah landscape. Book at El Questro's station store or via helispirit.com.au. I recommend pre-booking.

ZEBEDEE SPRINGS 39/100 ☐

Thermal springs in a Livistona palm tree oasis

Hot springs in the Kimberley? Yep, and they're some of the best you'll find in Australia. Tucked away amongst Livistona palms and beneath towering red cliffs, a series of thermal pools, created by water emerging from under a rock ledge, pour one into the next. The year-round 28 to 32°C waters spring from a sandstone Faultline, believed to originate from as far away as Papua New Guinea. Small waterfalls trickle between the rockpools, creating a sound akin to the kind of music you'd hear being played in a fancy day spa.

The easy 1.5km-return walk into Zebedee Springs is mostly flat, and this spot is definitely no secret. Unsurprisingly, this little oasis can pack a crowd, especially in the middle of the Dry Season. Arrive as soon as the gates open at 7 am for fewer people, as most campers are still getting up and eating their breakfast at this time. I recommend the pools at the very top, where there are fewer people. Just be careful when climbing up the slippery and (in places) sharp rocks; take it slow. The bigger, bottom pool is also lovely but beware of small leaches in there if you soak for too long.

El Questro's tourism operation was initially set up by an English bloke and his Aussie wife, Will and Celia Burrell, who gave this spot its name. Zebedee was a beloved cartoon character with the body of a coiled spring on the television show, *The Magic Roundabout*, which was popular in Britain during the 1960s and 70s. However, as El Questro's recently been returned from the Crown to its Traditional Owners, the Ngarinyin people, maybe Zebedee's British cartoon-inspired name will be replaced with a more Kimberley-appropriate one in future. Watch this space.

HIKES OF EL QUESTRO 40/100

01

Four of the best hikes in Ngarinyin country, southern El Questro

At 700,000 acres and with various accommodation options, El Questro is a favourite spot for travellers and Kununurra locals (like my family and me) looking for a quick and easy weekend getaway. The northern side of the Gibb River Road is the traditional country of the Balanggarra people. The scenery up there is dominated by the Cockburn Ranges, with Emma Gorge (page 112) recessed into them. The land on the southern side of the Gibb River Road is the traditional country of the Ngarinyin people. There are a handful of gorge walks to do in Ngarinyin country, but these are four of my favourites:

EL QUESTRO GORGE

McMicking Pool is the name of the small, fern-fringed swimming hole at the far end of El Questro Gorge. It was named after El Questro's original leaseholder, Torrance McMicking. Reaching McMicking Pool is a half-day endeavour, and though most crew come for this pool, there are some nice swims along the way. You'll set out by walking into a shady chasm and following a spring-fed creek for about an hour, before reaching a waterhole nicknamed Halfway Pool. Some folks turn around at this point. To continue to McMicking Pool, swim through the shallow water at Halfway Pool (pack your gear into a dry bag) and then clamber up to the top of the boulder on the left, continuing along the trail for another hour.

AMALIA GORGE

Lace up your hiking boots - you'll need them on this scenic but, at times, challenging hike. As one of El Questro's lesser-visited spots, Amalia Gorge is worth the walk, especially straight after the Wet Season rains when the waterfalls flow into the gorge pool at the end. Make sure you go for a swim despite the chilly water temperatures. Even without the waterfall, this gorge walk is spectacular.

Allow about two to three hours for this 3.4km return walk, leading you through rocky sections and along ledges you'll need to clamber across. The wall-hugging section may be a little nerve-racking, so make sure you're carrying a light load. The first swimming hole is about a third of the way along the track. It's worth jumping in to cool off, especially if you're coming later in the Dry Season when the gorge pool at the end may be stagnant. There's not much shade along this walk, so wear a hat, pack plenty of water and set out early in the morning (or in the afternoon) to avoid the midday sun.

CHAMPAGNE SPRINGS

Like Moonshine Gorge, Champagne Springs is challenging in some parts. Certainly, this is best earlier in the Dry Season before the pools slow down, but it's always worth it. The rocky, 9km return trail follows a creek, beginning with shady sections and a little climbing. At the halfway pool, there's a lovely opportunity for a swim. Unfortunately, the shade all but disappears on the second half of the trail, leaving you scrambling and rock-hopping along the escarpment. A sunrise start is recommended to avoid the hot midday sun. The pools at the end are beautiful, and the swimming hole is less popular than some of the easier ones in El Questro (like Zebedee Springs). Keep an eye out for snakes and the odd bullock along the river bank section.

MOONSHINE GORGE

This is a little-known hike in El Questro, and there are some difficult parts with sandy sections, creek crossings and boulder-lined riverbeds that just scream 'ankle injury'. Like the other hikes on these pages, wear the right shoes and take it slow. Plus, pack plenty of water and sun protection. The first part of the 4.7km loop walk is an old 4WD trail, and it's more user-friendly, with some shade (thanks to the cliffs and palm trees overhead). However, the trail gets more challenging in the second half when there is no shade. Thankfully, there are some pleasant opportunities to jump in and cool off at Moonshine Creek along the way, where it's likely that you'll only be sharing your swim with a couple of resident freshies and plenty of black bream. Some sections where the trail markers aren't obvious, so it is a good idea to chat with El Questro's tour desk staff before setting off.

01 McMicking Pool, El Questro Gorge
02 Amalia Gorge, early in the Dry Season

THE COCKBURN RANGE 41/100 ☐

A flat-topped escarpment, iconic to the east Kimberley

At the eastern end of the Gibb River Road, on Balanggarra country, is one of the Kimberley's most iconic natural landmarks – the Cockburn Range (pronounced co-burn). The predominant feature of this sandstone escarpment is its flat-top 'mesa' - the Spanish word for table.

The Cockburn Range was famously featured in Baz Luhrmann's film 'Australia' when King George stood on top of the plateau, singing out over the country. It's also the backdrop to just about every shot of off-roaders crossing the Pentecost River (page 104).

The plateau is heavily dissected with gorges and sheer cliffs towering 70 to 80m above. At the base of the cliffs are mudflats, ancient boab trees, tidal rivers and seemingly endless savannah landscapes. During Wet Season rains, hundreds of waterfalls spill from this escarpment, including King Falls – the tallest waterfall in Western Australia, plummeting more than 130m before flowing down into the King River. You only need to take a 30-minute chopper ride out of Kununurra for a birds-eye-view of this (and other waterfalls) during the Wet Season. Visit helispirit.com.au.

THE WEDDING TREE 42/100 ☐

A giant, old boab tree that's best visited at sunset

One of the best places to get a ripper boab tree photo in the east Kimberley is at the big, old boab that's been nicknamed 'The Wedding Tree' thanks to the many loved-up couples who have had wedding photos or fairytale-looking receptions here. But you don't need to get married to enjoy this spot.

Almost exactly halfway between the El Questro Station turn-off and the turn-off to Emma Gorge (GPS coordinates 15°54'59.0" S 128°04'55.4" E), you'll find the short access track into an area that often looks like it's been mowed. This is what makes it different from the many other boabs dotted within the Kimberley's savannahs – you can park directly across the dry creek to this one and walk around it without worrying about walking through head-high grasses. The backdrop of the Cockburn Range is especially lovely, and sunset is magic when it glows orange. BYO camp chairs, cheese and crackers.

Boabs are endemic to the Kimberley and the Northern Territory's Victoria River region. Every boab is unique and photo-worthy. To the Miriuwung people of the east Kimberley, they are called Gerdewoon, and they have been traditionally used for food, water, medicine and shelter for thousands of years. Their fruit is edible and high in vitamin C (with six times more vitamin C than an orange). Growing to 1,500 years and older, they are Australia's oldest living beings. Ancient Indigenous Dreamtime stories tell how the boab was once arrogant and proud, so the spirits plucked it from the earth and re-planted it upside-down. Amazingly, the native people of Madagascar have a similar traditional story for their baobab, a tree that is kin to the Australian boab and similar in appearance.

EMMA GORGE AND TURQUOISE POOL

43/100 ☐

An incredible sandstone amphitheatre one hour from Kununurra

To describe Emma Gorge in one word; breathtaking. As well as its natural beauty, anyone who's swum here will agree that the freshwater literally takes your breath away! Cold water is invigorating, but if you want to warm up, walk across to the right-hand side of the gorge, where a hot spring spills from a gap in the rocky platform, heating the waters below it to lukewarm.

Located within Balanggarra Country, on the northern side of the Gibb River Road (within El Questro Wilderness Park), the walk to the gorge begins at the Emma Gorge Resort. Allow an hour to reach the big swimming hole, fed by a spectacular, 65m-high, spring-fed waterfall.

Pack some lunch and something to float on, and plan to spend half a day here. The 3.2km return walk from Emma Gorge Resort's carpark has little shade and some slippery boulders to negotiate, so wear your good hiking boots, pack plenty of water

01 My wife, Taminga, enjoying the rare moment of having Emma Gorge all to ourselves

02 A small freshie in Turquoise Pool

03 Turquoise Pool under the midday sun

and avoid the midday sun. Allow about 45 minutes to an hour each way and set out well before 3 pm, as the day gets away quickly after that time and the trail is closed to hikers wanting to set off after then.

While Emma Gorge is the main attraction here, Turquoise Pool, 150m before the gorge, is worth a stop and a swim. When the mid-morning sun is overhead, this spot illuminates in an epic turquoise colour, hence the name. Keep an eye out for the small, resident freshies both here and in the gorge.

MITCHELL PLATEAU AND KALUMBURU

Intrepid explorers will be rewarded for their efforts to get to one of the most remote parts of the Kimberley, up one of its roughest roads. In this northern part of the Kimberley, there are tiered waterfalls, ancient rock art sites, breathtaking gorges and forests of Livistona palms. This country is wild, and there's a true sense of discovery for anyone who ventures up this way.

This is the traditional region of the Wunambal people, whose lineage and heritage have been unbroken for nearly 70,000 years. Despite leaving their lands under encouragement of government in the early part of the 20th century, they have eschewed the towns of the Kimberley for life on their own country since the 1980s. When the mining companies relinquished their leases to the state in 2012, the Wunambal people gained unquestioned possession of their lands. They continue in their long struggle for autonomy for their community and their future on Ngauwudu, Mitchell Plateau, and still hold high hopes of a thriving Kandiwal community.

Being so remote, it must be something pretty special to lure folks up here, and its most famous multi-tiered waterfall certainly doesn't disappoint. Deep in the heart of Wunambal country lies Punamii-Uunpuu, the Mitchell Falls. Travellers come by helicopter, light aircraft or 4WD to see the falls and those who drive here have the freedom to explore surrounding attractions, too, such as Surveyor's Pool (page 122) and the King Edward River (Munurru). Apart from the bushwalking and freshwater swimming at each of these spots, there's also the promise of discovering ancient Gwion Gwion (Bradshaw) art panels hidden in caves and often found near waterways. The newly created ranger base at Munurru campground is a fantastic place to purchase a guidebook on all the local artworks available to the public. The rock art in this region is the most spectacular you'll see by road anywhere in the Kimberley.

If you are driving, saddle up for a rough trip. Kalumburu Road is notoriously rough as the local council responsible for it simply doesn't have the resources to deal with the increasing levels of tourist traffic, wet season rains and general maintenance of such a remote strip of dirt. You will need a well-maintained 4WD and a healthy appreciation of corrugations. It can take hours, sometimes, just to travel 20km, especially if you are towing a caravan or trailer.

In general, I usually allow three to four hours to travel 160km from the Gibb River Road to the Mitchell Falls turnoff and another two or three hours for the last 86km to the falls, although it can sometimes be better (and sometimes much worse). It can take another four or five hours to get to Kalumburu. Stick to 40km/h on the Port Warrender Road to Mitchell Falls and 60km/h on Kalumburu Road, and you'll more likely get to your destination without breaking too much of your 4WD or trailer.

This part of the Kimberley gives me a true reverence for creation and raw nature. Having the coast feel so far away after a full day's drive, then suddenly getting a peep through the trees along the most inaccessible and untouched coastline in the world, you really feel this place on another scale to anything else you can experience in the Kimberley. People are forever asking me if it's worth it as they 'hear the roads really rough', and I'm forever answering that same question, yes, it is. Just do it!

Ancient Gwion Gwion (Bradshaw) art at Munurru (King Edward River)

0
20 kms
49
50
Uunguu Indigenous Protected Area
48
47
Lawley River National Park
44
45
46
MITCHELL PLATEAU
Laterite Conservation Park
KALUMBURU ROAD
Mitchell River National Park
Drysdale River National Park
Prince Regent National Park
Wilinggin Indigenous Protected Area
51
44 Mitchell Falls (Punamii-unpuu)
45 Little Mertens Falls (Bunjani)
46 King Edward River (Munurru)
47 Surveyors Pool (Aunauyu)
48 Kimberley Coastal Camp
49 Kalumburu's beach camps
50 Kalumburu's WW2 relics
51 Drysdale River Station

MITCHELL FALLS 44/100 ☐ (PUNAMII-UNPUU)

A four-tiered waterfall in the heart of Wunambal country

The Wunambal people know the four-tiered Mitchell Falls as Punamii-Unpuu, one of the Kimberley's most iconic landmarks and a place of great cultural and spiritual significance. Carved through sandstone by the Mitchell River, these faraway falls cascade 97m over four distinct tiers, each emerald pool flowing into the next.

In 2015, WA's state Premier announced that the plateau and the neighbouring Prince Regent and Lawley River National Parks would soon be known as Kimberley National Park: a five-million-hectare slice of pristine wilderness that would eclipse the Northern Territory's Kakadu as Australia's biggest ever sanctuary. Unfortunately, the plan was scrapped once a new government was voted in a few years later.

Access to the Mitchell Plateau (Ngauwudu) is via a long, corrugated and strictly 4WD-only gravel road. There's a campground run by WA's Parks and Wildlife Service or luxe safari tents at the Mitchell Falls Wilderness Lodge.

The 8.6km (return) walking trail to the falls is rated moderate to difficult, with patchy shade and some rock hopping. Start walking early to avoid the midday heat and to allow time to swim and explore Indigenous art along the way. Keep an eye out for wedge-tailed eagles, water monitors and little rock wallabies.

Swimming below the falls is not allowed, but there's great swimming in the river above. The walk to Mitchell Falls passes two other waterfalls: Little Mertens Falls and Mertens Gorge, an impressive waterfall unto itself. Beware when viewing Mertens Gorge as there's a steep 60m drop, and in 2012 a woman slipped and sadly fell to her death.

For access to Mitchell Falls and 12 other sites within Wunambal Gaambera Country, a five-day Uunguu Visitor Pass will set you back $45. Buy one online at wunambalgaambera.org.au.

01 Expert Kimberley guide, Kolya
02 The 60m falls at Mertens Gorge

LITTLE MERTENS FALLS (BUNJANI) 45/100 □

Rainforest, rock art, natural spa pools and a curtain waterfall

The little in Little Mertens Falls can be misleading, as this 15m waterfall is only small if it's compared to the mammoth waterfall at Mertens Gorge further along the track. While some think it is only a nice stop on the walk into Mitchell Falls, Little Mertens (Bunjani) is a worthy destination in its own right and one that you can quickly return to if you're camping at the nearby Mitchell Falls campground (1.6km return).

Leaving the Punamii-Unpuu Trail, a track leads you to the top of Little Mertens. You'll find numerous little spa pools within the rocky ledge that you can soak in. There's a nice view over the surrounding countryside, but I recommend walking down the steep track into the arena below. A track at the bottom leads behind the curtain of the waterfall and into a fern-lined cave. In the cave, rock walls showcase ancient Gwion Gwion (Bradshaw) art.

The best time to come is early morning when the tour groups are still eating breakfast. Keep an eye out for wildlife such as Mertens' water monitors and monjons – Australia's smallest rock wallaby. The monjon is so rare that it was only photographed for the very first time in 1985 (okay, maybe it's unlikely that you'll see a monjon, but you never know). When you sit quietly and watch the world moving around you for long enough, you'll see all kinds of things as the tour groups hurry straight past on their mission to get to Mitchell Falls.

KING EDWARD RIVER (MUNURRU)

Freshwater swimming and riverside camping

This beautiful river is the ultimate stopover point on your way to Mitchell Falls (Punamii-Unpuu). The river divides the traditional lands of the Ngarinyin and Wunambal peoples and is known to both as Munurru. The paperbark-fringed river is deep, clear, and perfect for refreshing dips and fishing.

There's a shady riverside campground managed by the Traditional Owners, and downstream, King Edwards Falls fills a picturesque rock amphitheatre that flows amber and gold at sunset. Take a walk to discover some of Australia's oldest rock art: Wandjina figures said to be 3,000 to 4,000 years old and ancient Gwion Gwion (Bradshaw) dancers and hunters depicted in intricate ceremonial scenes. For a bargain of $20 per person, you can join an Uunguu Ranger on a guided rock art tour by dropping into the Munurru Ranger Base, which includes a Welcome to Country. See wunambalgaambera.org.au for more information.

If you're planning on coming early in the Dry Season, the river can run too high to cross, so plan your trip from May onwards to be sure.

SURVEYORS POOL (AUNAUYU) 41/100 ☐

A pristine, relatively untouched location that's well worth a look

Continuing about 30km further north from the Mitchell Plateau turnoff, you'll find Surveyors Pool, known as Aunauyu to the Wunambal people. Following Port Warrender Road, you'll turn onto a rocky (and, at times, steep) 10km track, which leads to the parking area for Surveyors Pool, where a 1km (each way - allow about 30 mins) walk leads to the pool and waterfall.

To the Traditional Owners, the bottom pool is a sacred place, and they ask that visitors avoid swimming here. Plus, there may be saltwater crocs in that pool. But you'll find refreshing swimming and great views in the top pools above the fall. There are also some terrific rock art sites along the creek walls downstream, but please do not touch them and be very careful as you climb about, as the rocks are hazardous in places. Expect to scare a wallaby or two out of the shaded cool areas.

It's hard to get here, so there usually aren't many visitors, and you'll likely be swimming on your own. Unfortunately, there's no campsite, so your best bet is to head back to the Mitchell Plateau.

KIMBERLEY COASTAL CAMP 48/100 ☐

Fishing, rock art and fiery sunsets at this remote wilderness camp

Kimberley Coastal Camp is a remote beachside haven tucked away on the eastern edge of the Admiralty Gulf. The camp has rustic accommodation for just 16 guests at a time, and it is well known for its hospitable hosts, Tubs and Jules. Apart from the great fishing on offer, Tubs is highly knowledgeable about local Indigenous rock art. Jules is known for her incredible cook-ups incorporating fresh seafood like golden snapper, tiger prawns and mud crabs. She has even released her own cookbook, *Cooking in Thongs*.

The scenery here is stunning and pristine, the sunsets are on point, and there's great stargazing, thanks to the clear, dark skies in this remote location. The incredible fishing keeps many visitors busy. Off the water, there's rock art to discover and wildlife to spot. Keep an eye out for the endangered northern quoll.

This is the traditional country of the Wunambal Gaambera people, who call the area Yalrundair. The easiest way in is by chopper, boat or seaplane; Tubs and Jules will organise it as part of the package. Alternatively, you can drive to Port Warrender, and the crew will collect you by dinghy (by pre-arrangement) to cut out the cost of the air transfer.

September to May is best for barra fishing, June and July for bushwalking, beachcombing and crabbing, and March to May to enjoy the freshwater billabong after rain. Visit kimberleycoastalcamp.com.au or phone 0417 902 006.

KALUMBURU'S BEACH CAMPS

Fishing, camping and culture

Kalumburu and the nearby camps of Honeymoon Bay and McGowan Island Beach are the northernmost permanent settlements in Western Australia. Situated on the King Edward River, this area is rich in waterholes and Indigenous rock art sites, including Bradshaw paintings, known locally as Kira Kiro.

The area has traditionally been home to two distinct Aboriginal language groups, the Kwini (Kuini) and Kulari, although others have moved here in recent years. Catholic missionaries arrived in the early 1900s, and in 1939 Kalumburu became a strategic staging point during World War II.

While the Kalumburu community does have a campground, the coast is the place to be and the beach camps of Honeymoon Bay (27km north) and McGowan Island Beach (20km north) are worth the mission to get there. It's a bumpy and sandy track north of Kalumburu, so you'll need a high clearance 4WD. This is an excellent base for fishing or searching for swimming holes and WWII wrecks - with some directions from your camp hosts. BYO boat or, alternatively, Lancho at Honeymoon Bay offers fishing trips in his. Seek local advice before swimming anywhere in these parts. Visit honeymoonbaywa.com or facebook.com/McGowansSunsetBeachCampingWA. Check road conditions by calling ahead on (08) 9168 4100 or visiting swek.wa.gov.au.

A journey to Kalumburu is not for the faint-hearted. Due to its remote location, facilities are basic, and services are not cheap, as most goods arrive by barge from Darwin. It's best to bring your own fresh fruit and vegetables. Kalumburu is a dry community, meaning alcohol is prohibited. You can drink alcohol at the beach camps, but you must abide by some strict rules while passing through Kalumburu, including that you won't give (or sell) alcohol to any locals and that alcohol isn't visible from outside your car.

Access to Kalumburu requires a permit from the Aboriginal Lands Trust. Even if you're just passing through, you must get a permit. Apply online at dplh.wa.gov.au. A pass to stay or camp at Kalumburu is available on arrival from the Community Resource Centre or the Uraro Store. If Kalumburu is shut, you can also obtain a pass from Lancho and Joy at Honeymoon Bay.

01 Sunrise at Honeymoon Bay

02 Wandjina on a doorway at Kalumburu

03 Fishing with Lancho (far left)

KALUMBURU'S WWII RELICS

50/100 ☐

Relics from Kalumburu's time as a military outpost

Over the course of WWII, Japanese forces attacked Australian soil over 110 times. Some of the more famous attacks are well documented, especially around Broome, Darwin and Horn Island in the Torres Strait. Throughout the war effort, the tiny, remote Drysdale River Mission (now Kalumburu), which had its own airstrip, was used as an advanced refuelling and ammunition outpost so RAAF could conduct operations against the Japanese. As a result, it was bombed by Japanese forces on September 27, 1943, one of the last times Japanese aircraft entered Australian airspace during the war. Tragically, five Indigenous locals were killed (four children), along with one of the missionaries, who were all hiding in a makeshift bomb shelter.

Relics of Kalumburu's use as a military outpost are still scattered throughout town. The Kalumburu Mission Museum in town is a great place to start, and the caretakers will tell stories of the town's history.

Driving out to the old airstrip behind the current airport is fascinating. Although the strip has been taken back by nature, here lies the wrecks of Airforce DC3 bombers damaged in the raid (one has been shipped off to a museum down south for restoration, and another had to be blown up by Aussie forces to move it off the airstrip after the attack!). Like so many of the destroyed or crashed air force planes scattered around Australia's north, you can climb in and out of them and walk around the site unhindered by fences or cordons.

While you're north of town, or on the way to the beach camps, you can stop off for a swim and a bit more history at Anscar

Rock and Turtle Rock, or just for a swim. Anscar Rock is named after the Benedictine Missionary Father Anscar McFee, who dedicated his life to the small community until he died in 2008. The locals consider it a safe swimming spot (but check with them first). If you take a wander, you'll be able to find some local rock art sites. Turtle Rock, a little further north, is so called because of the striking resemblance one high-perched rock has to a turtle. The pool here is fern-fringed and the perfect place to cool off. Both are signed a few kilometres north of town, and a walking circuit connects them.

DRYSDALE RIVER STATION 51/100 □

01

Great food, a swimming hole and light aircraft flights to the Mitchell Falls

One million acres and running about 700 head of cattle, Drysdale River Station breaks up the drive from the Gibb River Road to the Mitchell Plateau. It offers camping, basic accommodation, and hearty pub-style meals (book ahead for dinner during the Dry Season). An added bonus is a nice freshwater swimming hole called Miner's Pool (no camping). It got its name from its use as a permanent campsite for mining explorers during the early 1980s.

Today operated by the Koeyers family, who took up the pastoral lease in 1985, Drysdale has an interesting history. Perhaps its most famous leasee was Captain Joseph Bradshaw, who, while trying to reach some of his pastoral leases on the Prince Regent River in 1891, first saw and recorded the mysterious rock art now known as Bradshaw Art or Gwion Gwion. After that expedition, Bradshaw was unable to find them again. They remained unknown to the outside world until 1996 when Grahame Walsh found a painting under a fossilised mud wasp nest. First edition copies of Walsh's book *Bradshaw Art of the Kimberley* now sell for over $4,000.

These days, Drysdale River Station is well known for its excellent outback hospitality, and it's also the last spot to buy fuel before the Mitchell Plateau. The station

02

offers tyre repairs, including new tyres and tubes, which is helpful in this part of the world where the road is notoriously bad. There are basic cabins and a dog-friendly campground with hot showers. Unfortunately, due to many no-shows in the past, Drysdale no longer takes advance bookings for campsites. The campsite is huge, so there's nearly always space, and the team rarely turn people away. Pay at the station's shop, which is open from 8 am until 5 pm each day (it generally gets dark around 5.30 pm, so you'll want to be off the road by this time, anyway).

Drysdale River Station is 59km north of the Gibb River and Kalumburu Roads' junction. The Traditional Owners of the area are the Ngarinjin, Miwa and Wilawila people. There's an airstrip where light aircraft flights to the Mitchell Falls are on offer, usually from May until the end of August, which is excellent for those who want to check out the falls but avoid the big drive in. For information on camping, scenic flights and more. Check out drysdaleriver.com.au.

01 Miner's Pool

02 One of Drysdale's famous hamburgers

03 Take a scenic flight to the Mitchell Falls from Drysdale River Station

03

KUNUNURRA AND THE EAST KIMBERLEY

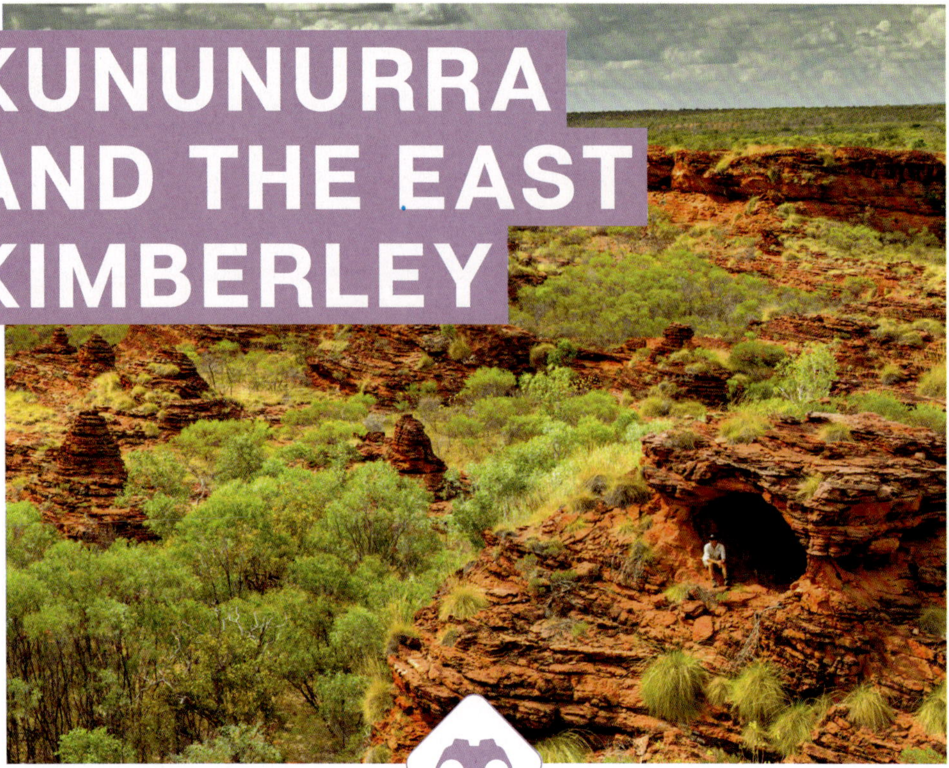

In the far east of the Kimberley, just 37km shy of the Western Australia/Northern Territory border, is the town of Kununurra. For me, this is my favourite chapter to write in this book, as this region is my home. I operate my safaris from here, and my wife, Taminga, gains great inspiration from the surrounding country for her paintings.

I moved from Broome to Kununurra in the early 2000s after discovering how amazing the Ord River is for wakeboarding. The freshwater is soothing, and I love the lifestyle amongst the mountains. There is just so much to do; from my favourite local swimming spots, such as Swim Beach in Kununurra, to the many waterholes just out of town, which are a mixture of Wet Season waterfalls and year-round spring-fed pools.

Kununurra is the traditional country of the Miriuwung Gajerrong people, who are freshwater people, and much of their art reflects that connection to the water. Most of the local Indigenous art is painted with natural ochres that communicate a strong connection with country, despite many Indigenous peoples having been forced off their land during the development of the pastoral industry and Ord irrigation scheme. I recommend checking out the galleries in Kununurra or dropping into Waringarri Arts , which is Indigenous-owned and supports the work of over 100 local Indigenous artists.

Kununurra's history is rich and varied and worth delving into. Start at the Kununurra Museum on Coolibah Drive. Operation Ord Noah is a fascinating collection of photos from the 1971-72 Wet Season when Lake Argyle first began to flood with water. The Western Australian Wildlife Association conducted a mammoth operation to relocate as much wildlife as possible. The photo of Harry Butler gripping onto the side of a tinny, neck-deep in water, while holding a king brown shows the level of commitment from the volunteers. It's open on weekdays from 12.30 pm to 5.30 pm (depending on the availability of volunteers). kununurra.org.au.

While the Argyle Dam feeds a year-round water supply to the surrounding farmlands via the Ord River, many people don't know that it also provides electricity to Kununurra and Wyndham. You'll see the Ord hydro plant at the base of Argyle's dam wall. This is a great place to spot freshwater crocs.

Beyond the water, there are plenty of ways to explore the countryside of the east Kimberley. Just on the outskirts of Kununurra's CBD is Mirima National Park (page 146), which is worth a hike at sunrise or sunset when the rocks are glowing. And, like all great country towns, there are some local characters with yarns to tell to those who will listen. Some have been running small businesses here for many years, such as Greg from Lake Argyle Cruises (page 160) or Mandy from Kangaroo Haven (page 147). Ben Ward at Waringarri is a great storyteller who lived on Argyle Downs before it was flooded. Others will tell their stories through art; some are painted on canvases, and some are carved into boab nuts. You'll find that most people that have lived here for a while have a good story to tell. Hang around for long enough, and you'll leave with a few good stories, too.

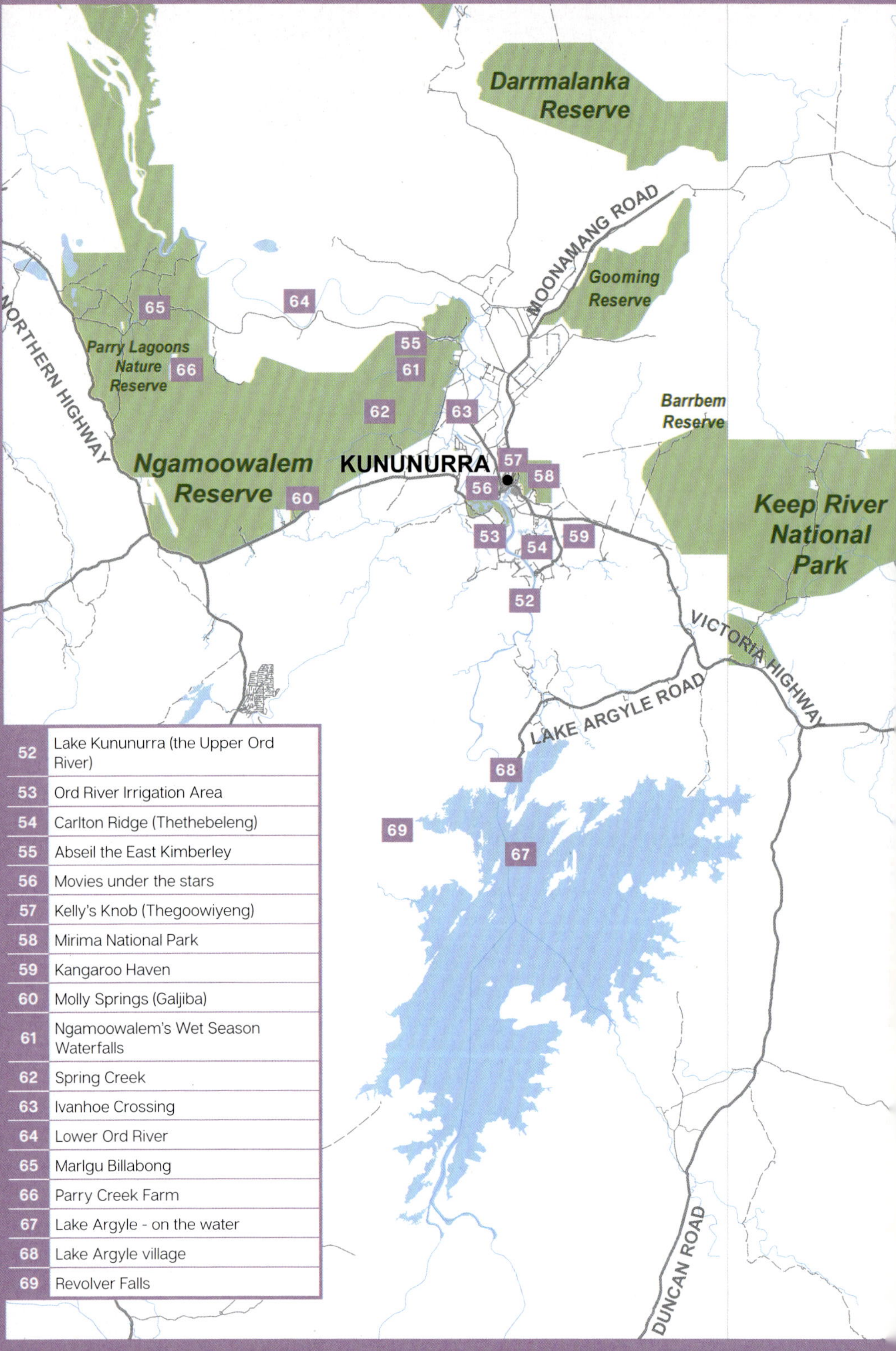

52	Lake Kununurra (the Upper Ord River)
53	Ord River Irrigation Area
54	Carlton Ridge (Thethebeleng)
55	Abseil the East Kimberley
56	Movies under the stars
57	Kelly's Knob (Thegoowiyeng)
58	Mirima National Park
59	Kangaroo Haven
60	Molly Springs (Galjiba)
61	Ngamoowalem's Wet Season Waterfalls
62	Spring Creek
63	Ivanhoe Crossing
64	Lower Ord River
65	Marlgu Billabong
66	Parry Creek Farm
67	Lake Argyle - on the water
68	Lake Argyle village
69	Revolver Falls

LAKE KUNUNURRA (THE UPPER ORD RIVER) 52/100 ☐

Canoe with fresh water crocs on this glorious 55km waterway

The Eastern Kimberley is a place of many rivers. In fact, the name Kununurra means river, having been derived from the Miriuwung word 'Goonoonoorrang'.

Bookended by Lake Argyle upstream and the Diversion Dam downstream, Lake Kununurra and the Upper Ord River supply irrigation to surrounding farms, while the hydroelectric power station at the base of the Ord Dam supplies renewable energy to Kununurra and Wyndham. The lake is also a wildlife haven, home to thousands of freshwater crocs and hundreds of bird species, including rainbow bee-eaters and jabirus (black-necked stork).

For Kununurra locals, the river is a playground for boating, fishing and Wet Season waterfall hunting. Fancy a swim with a few thousand freshies? Swim Beach is the place to be, with a sandy bottom and a rope swing over the water. Driving towards Kununurra's CBD, take your first right after crossing the Diversion Dam and park under a shady mango tree near the toilets (so your steering wheel isn't searing hot after your swim).

If you'd rather be on the water than in the water, boating the Ord is a popular option.

Triple J Tours offers day cruises down the full length of the Upper Ord from Lake Argyle, including the breathtaking Carlton Gorge – triplejtours.com.au. Alternatively, and highly recommended by myself, is Go Wild Adventure Tours' canoe trips, owned by the legend Adam 'Maka' Mackay. Maka offers one- or three-day canoe trips with riverside camps along the way. Highlights of the canoe trips include swimming in the river from a couple of the sandy beaches, hiking up hills to find freshwater spring-fed waterholes, jumping from the 'jump rock,' Carlton Gorge and sleeping under the stars (if you've opted for an overnight trip). The three-day canoe trips are the most popular, from $290 per person, including camping gear. gowild.com.au

01 Canoeing through Carlton Gorge
02 Jump Rock

ORD RIVER 53/100 ☐ IRRIGATION AREA

The valley of fresh food dreams

Speak with any Miriuwung Elder who lived in Kununurra before the damming of the Ord, and they'll tell you about the permanent waterhole where everyone used to hunt and gather called Carlton Reach, held back by the Bandicoot Bar. This is now the site of the Diversion Dam, one of the township's most prominent features. It separates freshwater Lake Kununurra (the upper Ord River) from the lower part of the river, eventually turning to tidal saltwater just north of Wyndham.

In 1941, Before the dam was built, the Western Australian government set up a small farm on the Ord. Although this experimental farm failed, the government wouldn't abandon the idea of using the region for farming. Despite the vast amount of annual rain that Kununurra receives (about 800mm), most of it falls during just a few months of The Wet, making agriculture near-impossible. Eventually, the WA government was able to convince the federal government to split the cost of a dam, and between 1959 and 1962, the Diversion Dam was built, with Kununurra gazetted as a townsite in 1961.

Opened in 1963, its completion guaranteed a controlled flow of water from the man-made Lake Argyle. Water held within the 55km-long Lake Kununurra gravity-feeds the irrigation channels of the Ord River Irrigation Area (ORIA), providing fresh water to crops like mangoes, sandalwood, melons, cotton and more. Twenty radial gates within the Diversion Dam release water from Lake Kununurra into the Lower Ord, which then flows into Wyndham's Cambridge Gulf.

There's food everywhere you look around Kununurra, both bush food and food grown within the irrigation area. And you can shop directly from the farmers for the freshest, seasonal produce. For full-flavoured bananas, head to Reach Beyond across the Diversion Bridge at the start of Packsaddle Road. Or, closer to town, head down Riverfarm Road to pick up seasonal produce like papaya, honey, zucchini, squash and cucumbers from local sellers' honesty boxes. In Kununurra's CBD, Kimberley Cafe and the IGA Tuckerbox sell local produce, including frozen mango (yum). Opposite the Tuckerbox is Whitegum Park, where the local markets are held each Saturday from 8 am until noon during the Dry Season months of May to September. You can buy fresh, local produce from the farms directly at the markets. You can also grab a fresh mango ice cream or some local Thai food while you're at it.

01 Irrigation channels on Ivanhoe Road
02 The Diversion Dam

CARLTON RIDGE 54/100 ☐ (THETHEBELENG)

Float on the river in front of Elephant Rock to see the colours change

Standing guard over Lake Kununurra is the iconic Carlton Ridge, best viewed while boating the upper Ord River or from Packsaddle Road. It has gained the nickname 'Elephant Rock' because, when viewed from the front, the rock resembles an elephant's head, with a ridge down the rock face forming the trunk. To the Miriuwung people, this is Thethebeleng.

A sunrise climb rewards with breathtaking views over the glassy river, wetlands and surrounding countryside and takes about 30 minutes each way. Good walking shoes are a must due to slippery rocks and steep sections. Prepare for some off-track improvisation, as there is no official walking trail. The best way is to either hitch a ride with a local in their dinghy to the base of the rock (make sure they join you, so you can hitch a ride back after your hike) or grab a boat from Lake Kununurra Boat Hire, see lkboathire.com.au. If you're paddling the river in one of Maka's canoes (page 137), pull up at one of the rock bars in line with the back of the elephant's head and begin your hike from there. You'll know you're at the right place if it's flat enough for you to be able to pull your canoe up onto it. There's a deep V section of crumbled rocks running up the side of the elephant (just past the

01 I recommend kayaking through Emu Creek Wetlands, behind the rock

02 From the front, it looks like an elephant

03 Hike to the top to watch the sunrise

back of the elephant's head) – aim for that area, but watch your footing and keep an eye out for snakes. There is no official track, so the best option is to go with a local. There is also a way to climb the ridge from the back of the rock, near the pistol club, but vehicle access is limited and takes much longer. Do it at your own risk.

Rock art can be seen at the base of the rock, at the very southern end near Emu Creek Wetlands. Also, the bird life in this area is spot on. You will likely see rainbow bee-eaters, Azure kingfishers and pelicans. Early mornings and late evenings are a real treat, although you can hear a fantastic chorus of nature enjoying this special spot at any time of the day.

ABSEIL THE EAST KIMBERLEY

Dangle like a spider over the edge of a gorge

Imagine slowly inching your way over the edge of the 75m drop that is Black Rock Falls, one of the east Kimberley's most incredible rock faces and the host to a glorious Wet Season waterfall (see page 151). This is just one of the spectacular locations that local adventurer Maka of Go Wild Adventure Tours has been offering to adrenaline junkies since he started operations in 1997. What an incredible way to experience the Kimberley's iconic landscape.

If the 'massive jumps with max air time' of Black Rock are a little intimidating, there are some starter (less scary) options up the Ord River. Jump Rock, a favourite spot for boaties to cool off for a swim, is only 24m. This rock is also a favourite for locals and canoers to scale up one of the smaller ledges and take a thrilling jump into the warm waters of the river below. Cruising to this part of the river is an excellent opportunity to check out the Ord by boat and venture through the spectacular walls of Carlton Gorge.

If you'd like to try your hand at abseiling, Maka charges a flat group rate from $600 for half a day for a group of two to ten people to split between each other. So, either hustle together a group or call Maka and put your name down to join other individuals that may be keen. Check out gowild.com.au/abseiling for the full range of abseils on offer.

MOVIES UNDER THE STARS

Watch new releases the old way, outdoors

One of the greatest ways to enjoy a night under the stars in the east Kimberley is in the outdoor picture gardens. Both Kununurra and Wyndham have them, where you can watch the stars on the big screen and keep an eye out for shooting stars overhead!

It's rare to find an outdoor movie theatre these days, which makes the three in the Kimberley so special (there's also one in Broome - Sun Pictures in Chinatown). Community-owned and volunteer-run, Kununurra Picture Gardens and Wyndham Picture Gardens operate on weekends from March to November (weather permitting). For the latest schedules, see kpg.org.au for Kununurra or wyndhampicturegardens.com.au for Wyndham.

Get to the gates early, as there's often a line. If you're fortunate enough to have a ute, throw your couch or beanbags on the tray and reverse into your spot. Alternatively, BYO camping chair and grab a seat up front, closer to the screen. You can bring your own food, but there are great little kiosks at both cinemas. Expect a full house for the more popular latest releases, especially in the middle of the Dry Season. And remember your insect repellent!

KELLY'S KNOB 57/100 ☐ (THEGOOWIYENG)

Enjoy great views over Kununurra and Mirima

At 191m above the surrounding countryside, the highest point in Kununurra is Kelly's Knob lookout, just on the edge of the town centre, between the industrial area and Mirima National Park. From here, you can also see the Ord Valley in its entirety, as well as Mirima National Park and its surrounding terrain. You'll also be at eye level with soaring birds of prey, such as osprey and whistling kites.

This spot gets its name from Catholic priest Father Kelly, but the Indigenous name is Thegoowiyeng. If you'd like to learn more about the local Miriuwung culture, drop into Waringarri Aboriginal Arts on Speargrass Road, just opposite the turn-off onto Kelly Road. Waringarri closes at 4.30 pm, which

01 Hike to the top of the rocky outcrop for glorious views over Kununurra

02 Join a sunset tour with Ted Carlton. Book through Waringarri Arts

is perfect timing to browse the gallery and then head across the road for a sunset hike to the lookout.

To get there, turn onto Kelly Road and drive up the hill for about 500m until you come to the carpark at the end. From there, you'll find a shorter, five-minute walk to a lookout on your right, but head left through the gate for the walk to the top.

Sunrise or sunset are the best times to come, mainly to avoid the midday heat. Either way, you'll work up a sweat while climbing up to the top lookout, which is about 20 minutes each way. It's a challenging walk, so wear good shoes and carry a bottle of water. Once you've made it to the silver staircase, keep going, as you're almost at the top! This climb is a winner for incredible vistas and a good workout without paying to go to the gym.

MIRIMA NATIONAL PARK 58/100 ☐

The mini Bungles, right on the edge of Kununurra's CBD

Mirima National Park (also called Hidden Valley) is so close to Kununurra's town centre you can walk there. Here, you'll find great walking trails and lookouts which showcase stunning views of the Ord Valley.

The national park is often referred to as 'the mini Bungles' due to the similarity between the tiger-striped outcrops found here and in Purnululu National Park, 300km south (read more about it on page 174). Sacred to the Miriuwung people, Mirima has long provided shelter, water, food, medicine, and a place to perform ceremonies. I recommend joining a local Indigenous guide from Waringarri Aboriginal Arts, who offer half an hour walking tours through Mirima for $85 per person (adult) or $45 for kids 5-15 years old. See waringarriarts.com.au.

It's an amazing feeling to meander through this ancient landscape and quietly observe the flora and fauna that characterises such a beautiful part of Australia. There are designated walking trails with signposts and scenic lookouts, and a wheelchair-friendly boardwalk, toilet and BBQ area near the central carpark.

Keep an eye out for agile and short-eared rock wallabies that like to hide amongst the rocks. Lily Creek is a great spot to look for flighty double-barred and crimson finches. Arrive at sunrise or sunset to see the park at its best, avoiding the middle of the day (because it gets quite hot). A $15 per vehicle national park entrance fee is payable if you intend to drive to the carpark where the trails begin. Come during Wet Season rainfall (usually between December to March) to see the park transform with waterfalls and normally-hidden springs spilling from the rocks.

KANGAROO HAVEN 59/100 ☐

Bottlefeed a joey and meet some cute sugar gliders

What happens to kangaroos and wallabies that get injured by cars in the eastern Kimberley? They end up in the 10-acre backyard of Mandy Watson at Egret Close, about ten minutes on the highway east of Kununurra. Kangaroo Haven is Mandy's not-for-profit wildlife rescue, which she's operated with the help of other passionate volunteers for over 15 years.

For Mandy, it all began when she and her partner hit a red kangaroo and rescued the joey from its pouch. Since then, they have successfully released over 650 wallabies and 'roos back into the wild.

For a donation of $15 per person (or more, if you're feeling generous), Mandy will introduce you to some of her rescued wildlife. She may even share a funny story or two about the time Aussie comedians Hamish and Andy dropped by.

On your visit to Kangaroo Haven, you'll meet rescued wildlife, including sugar gliders, emus and, yes, wallabies and 'roos. You may even get to hold a baby joey and bottlefeed it, like Mandy is in this photo.

Book via kangaroohavenwildliferescue.com.au or phone 0438 921 942 with at least 24 hours' notice. Some days can get especially busy, so when you're booking, ask Mandy which day has the fewest bookings.

MOLLY SPRINGS (GALJIBA) 60/100 ☐

A small, spring-fed waterhole, 20 minutes from Kununurra

There are plenty of great swimming holes in the eastern Kimberley, though many tend to dry up after the last of the Wet Season rains (usually from May). Thankfully, this one's a beauty and it's not too far from Kununurra.

Located within the Ngamoowalem Conservation Reserve, 30km west of Kununurra via the Victoria Highway, Molly Springs is a tiny waterhole that is a favourite for locals and visitors alike. Being spring-fed, Molly Springs doesn't dry up, and you can expect a small waterfall at the start of the Dry Season, which reduces to a trickle before it rains again later in the year. The swimming hole is barely big enough to do three or four breaststrokes across, so it can feel crowded when there are more than five people there. Arrive early in the morning to skip the crowds.

There's plenty of shade around the waterhole, as well as some small plunge pools above the tiny waterfall. For the Miriuwung people, it's a culturally significant site as they used to camp here and hunt goannas and kangaroos. They would get their fix of sweets from the sugarbag (honey) in the hollow trunks of surrounding Eucalyptus minata (Woollybutt trees), which provide a home for native, non-stinging bees.

Access is via a dirt track, though you can drive a 2WD vehicle in if you take it slow. Look for the track to your right (and a sign) just after Weaner Creek on the Victoria Highway.

STAY

It's all about being on the water in this part of the Kimberley, and below are a few great waterfront options.

Kimberleyland and Maxwells Camp are both situated on Lake Kununurra, so you can conveniently jump into the freshwater at any time for a cool off. Otherwise, head down to the free camp at Buttons Crossing. But, no swimming, salties live here! For a grand view, the holy grail of campsites is Lake Argyle (page 162). The infinity pool here is potentially the best you'll find in a campground.

BUTTONS CROSSING

The Lower Ord is as wild as it gets; giant salties, bat colonies, barra and untamed wilderness. After driving over Ivanhoe Crossing, continue north for ten minutes, and you'll find Buttons Crossing, with lots of shady spots. This popular free camp can get busy. If there are no spots, head to Mambi Island free camp, off Parry Road. You won't find it on a map, so here are the coordinates 15° 34' 58" S 128° 28' 23.98" E.

KIMBERLEYLAND

Owned and managed by locals Chris and Maria Magnay (I recommend reading Maria's mum's book A Diamond in the Dust'), Kimberleyland Waterfront Holiday Park is right on Lake Kununurra and is also locally loved for its great coffee at Spilled The Beans Cafe. The community vibe here is strong and very welcoming. Book via kimberleyland.com.au

MAXWELLS CAMP

If you don't need power or mobile phone coverage, this leafy campsite on the Ord River is an absolute winner. Run by Maka of Go Wild Adventure Tours, it's used for his canoe trips (page 137), but there are extra campsites. No caravans and no generators here. High clearance vehicles only that aren't too tall. Visit gowild.com.au/maxwell-camp

NGAMOOWALEM'S WET SEASON WATERFALLS 61/100 ☐

01

These waterfalls pump straight after Wet Season rainfall

Ngamoowalem (Na-moo-wal-eum) is a conservation reserve west of Kununurra and home to many gorges and springs. It is especially spectacular during the Wet Season, straight after rainfall. This reserve is a culturally significant place for the Miriuwung people with ceremonial sites, paintings and artefacts.

On the far eastern edge of the reserve, Valentine Spring Road is a wide (and often corrugated) dirt track that leads away from the highway, 10km from Kununurra. It travels northward, running adjacent to the Lower Ord River before becoming Parry Creek Road. After Wet Season rainfall, you'll find a series of pumping waterfalls along Valentine Spring Road. You can also get here over Ivanhoe Crossing (page 154), but heavy rain usually means that the crossing and Valentine Spring Road will both be closed. Each of the following waterholes is great straight after the Wet, but then they stagnate as the Dry Season continues.

VALENTINE SPRING (BARNDABA)

Valentine Spring (Barndaba) is the first spot, and you can pull your 4WD straight up to the waterhole. While locals often swim here, salties can get into this swimming hole, so be mindful and swim in the rapids above, where you can see the bottom.

MIDDLE SPRING (MAYIBA)

Continuing north, you'll find the turn-off to Middle Spring (Mayiba), a large swimming hole with a cascading, seasonal waterfall. Travel 2.2km down a narrow dirt track, and if you're willing to cross the last little water body, you can pull up straight in front of the waterhole. This spot is a beauty!

BLACK ROCK FALLS (THEGOOYENG)

From Middle Spring, you can bush bash via a 1.2km 4WD track up to Black Rock Falls (Thegooyeng) or head back to Valentine Spring Road again and drive around to find an easier track (4WD still required). Black Rock is one of my personal favourites. It's a 75m high waterfall with a dark-coloured rock face stained by minerals in the water, making it unique amongst the red gorges of the Kimberley. When the waterfall's flowing, this spot is absolute magic! If you don't have a 4WD, you can join Kingfisher Tours' six-hour Waterfall Wanderer tour for $350 per person at kingfishertours.com.au.

01 Black Rock Falls (Thegooyeng)
02 Valentine Spring (Barndaba)
03 Middle Spring (Mayiba)

SPRING CREEK 62/100 ☐

Permanent, spring-fed pools, cascading down a hillside

Locally known as Secret Springs, these permanent spring-fed pools are now signposted and on Google maps, but visitors take note: unless you have a high clearance 4WD and recovery gear, don't attempt this track. On that same note, if you see someone else that's stuck, jump out and give them a hand. Prepare for about 45 minutes (each way) of water crossings, washouts, potholes and sections with large boulders for your tyres to crawl across slowly.

If you're confident to give it a go, prepare for one of the east Kimberley's finest swimming spots, with pristine waterfalls cascading down a hillside, each pool pouring into the next. If you're feeling adventurous, skip the popular bottom swimming hole and carefully climb up to the top pools for incredible views and fewer people. Perhaps

the best part is that this waterhole is swimmable year-round, without stagnating or the falls drying up, as it's spring-fed. This place is good soul fuel.

To get to Spring Creek, follow Valentine Spring Road into the Ngamoowalem Conservation Reserve until you see the clearly-marked sign for Spring Creek. You will pass Middle Spring, Black Rock and Buttons Crossing turn-offs, and it's about another 15 minutes north. You can also come from the north, driving from Marlgu Billabong and Wyndham on the Parry Creek Road, although this way does take a bit longer via a bumpy and sharp-rocked dirt road. If you don't have a 4WD, or you'd rather not get your car scratched and dented (on my last trip out here, I lost my number plate in one of the water crossings), you can ask at the Kununurra Visitor Centre for an available local tour operator who you can jump on a trip with.

IVANHOE CROSSING 63/100 ☐

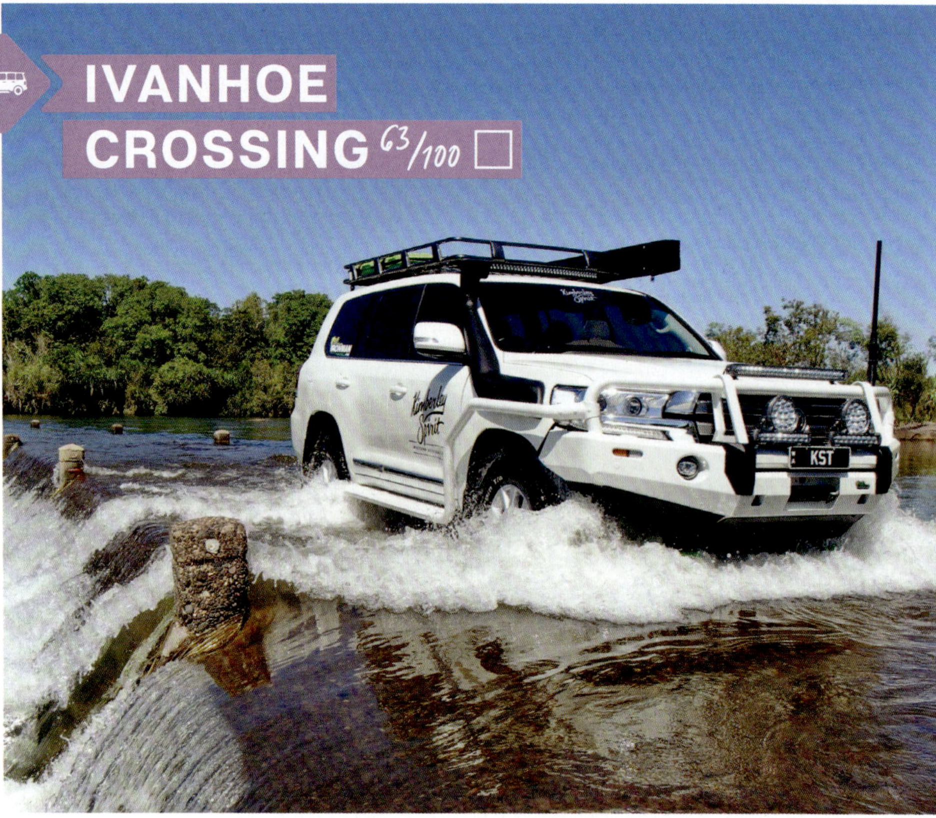

The old road across the Ord to Wyndham

Now a popular spot for local fishermen, this concrete causeway was once part of the main road between Kununurra and Wyndham. The crossing was initially built to service the northern township before Kununurra even existed.

Workers toiled over two Dry Seasons to build it, and the 750 disused 44-gallon drums that were the main construction materials remain in place today. The road was flooded when the Ord Irrigation Scheme began in the 1960s, creating a favourite spot for locals to flick a line for barra into the turbulent waters below the crossing. If you're thinking of casting a line alongside the locals, beware; saltwater crocs inhabit these waters and are never too far away from the crossing, whether you can see them or not.

It's fun to drive across the river these days, which is possible only during the Dry Season when water levels drop. The gate just before the crossing will be closed when the water level is too high. On the northern side, Parry Creek Road leads to some scenic spots, including Marlgu Billabong (page 158) or the waterfalls mentioned on pages 150 and 152. Due to the strong undercurrents of the causeway, a 4WD vehicle is required. If you're not up for braving the crossing, grab a seat on top of the stone Ivanhoe Crossing sign, which offers the ultimate vantage point to photograph vehicles crossing over.

EAT

With all of the fresh produce grown in the Ord valley and in the bush around Kununurra, there are some great options for finding yourself some tucker about these parts.

The ones that I've mentioned below are some local favourites, and each of them caters to various dietary needs. Remember, Kununurra is a remote and seasonal town, so expect that goods and services may come at a premium and (due to staff shortages) service can be slow sometimes.

KIMBERLEY CAFE

Tucked away on Papuana Street - a side street in the centre of Kununurra's CBD - Kimberley Cafe has a good country vibe and a florist that sells freshly cut flowers. Their fresh juices are fantastic and there is plenty of seating inside, with memorabilia from all over the Kimberley giving it a distinct charm.

IVANHOE CAFE

Pull up a seat under one of the mango trees and give Gromit, their pet Labrador a pat. Open from May to September, Ivanhoe Cafe is known for its mango smoothies, fresh pumpkin salads, homemade sausage rolls, pies and, one of my favourites, the pulled pork burger. Their breakfasts are good, too.

HOOCHERY DISTILLERY

Walk through the saloon doors for award-winning rums, homemade cakes or even a Wyndham Barra Taco from Western Australia's oldest, continuously operating legal still. The cafe is open from May to September, but the cellar door and rum tasting are year-round. hoochery.com.au.

LOWER ORD RIVER 64/100 □

Barra fishing in Jurassic Park

Good things come to those who bait. But if you're planning on catching live bait, beware, this is the saltie's lair! The Lower Ord is a popular spot for barra fishing, but it's also home to plenty of saltwater crocodiles (Crocodylus porosus), some of which are huge!

The traditional country of the Miriuwung Gajerrong peoples, the Lower Ord, is wild. The surrounding landscape is spectacular, with mangrove forests, lagoons, creeks and extensive floodplains. An adventure on the Lower Ord feels like stepping back in time, with almost zero development and thriving, untouched ecosystems. To experience this country, joining local fishing tour operator, Northbound Charters, for a half- or full-day trip down the Ord is your best bet. They take nice, small groups of four guests at the most - see northboundcharters.com.au. Alternatively, dedicated anglers can join

Mick from Kimberley Barra Tours, based out of John and Jo's camp (formally known as Macca's Barra Camp). Mick's a top bloke with extensive knowledge of the history and surrounding area, and he can land a barra with the best of them. Phone 0475 469 773.

For overnight camping down the Lower Ord, head to Ultimate Adventure's camp, which has unpowered sites available for you to set up at or, if you're on one of their extended tours, they have rustic, bush-camp accommodation included. See barramundiadventures.com.au. This is about an hour's drive from up the old Wyndham Road (Parry Creek Road) from Kununurra. Alternatively, check out the popular free camp at Button's Creek - there's more information on page 149.

01 Elise Cook lands her first barra

02 Keep your limbs inside the boat at all times!

MARLGU BILLABONG

A bird watcher's paradise

Are you an avid twitcher or just a wildlife lover like me? Well, you'll love Marlgu Billabong. To the local Miriuwung and Gajerrong people, the meaning of Marlgu is 'wild bird,' and there certainly is plenty to see here.

Perched on the edge of the Ord River floodplain within the RAMSAR-protected Parry Creek Nature Reserve, half of the fun is getting here. (But be aware that Wet Season rains may cut access roads). 4WD the old route from Kununurra to Wyndham along Parry Creek Road to get to Marlgu Billabong. Here, a short track leads to a shaded platform overlooking the water. If you get your timing right, you'll spot many species of bird congregating together, with the occasional saltwater croc lurking beneath the surface. Over 160 species of birds have been recorded at Marlgu Billabong, including magpie geese, cranes, brolga, jabiru, black swans and 17 different varieties of duck. The billabong is a stopping place for migratory waders from as far away as Siberia.

Dusk or dawn are the best times to visit. Near Telegraph Hill, you'll discover a fantastic spot to watch the sunset after seeing the billabong. Here you'll find the ruins of an old telegraph station built in 1914 and used during World War I. It's certainly a strange sight to see historical ruins in such a remote location.

PARRY CREEK FARM

Great food and camping

When Parry Creek Farm sold in early 2022, there was some apprehension over the future of this nature retreat, loved by both locals and travellers, many of whom are repeat guests. But thankfully, the new owners (Mark and Michelle) have breathed life into this institution, upgrading the caravan park and renovating the restaurant.

20km from Wyndham and situated within Parry Lagoons Nature Reserve, Parry Creek Farm is the closest accommodation to the northern part of the Gibb River Road, and it's just 12km away from Marlgu Billabong. Overlooking a picturesque lagoon, there are lovely treetop cabins that are connected by an elevated boardwalk. There's also a campground that's suitable for both tents and caravans and, best of all (according to my border collie, Fly), it's dog friendly.

While it can be hard to spot wildlife in the savannahs of the Kimberley, waterways are often a great place to look, and, at Parry's, over 200 species have been identified, including the rare Gouldian Finch. Look for birds in the reeds around the lagoon beneath the boardwalk, or head down to the back of the property and across the creek bed into the floodplains. Always be careful around waterways, as saltwater crocs can be found here. One good spot to look for them is Alligator Hole, now known as Crocodile Hole. You might spot crocs on the sandbanks or stealthily peeking out from the water. This spot is 10km along the Old Halls Creek Gold Rush Track, which begins at Parry Creek Farm. This track was originally built by prisoners in the late 1800s and used by gold miners to push their carts to the goldfields.

Parry Creek Farm is worthy of staying for a few nights to soak up the Kimberley hospitality and explore the surrounding scenery of Wyndham, the Lower Ord River and (of course) the surrounding nature reserve. But, you can also come here as a day visitor and enjoy the newly renovated kitchen and Fusion Restaurant for lunch or dinner; reservations are recommended during the Dry Season, especially on the weekends. Visit parrycreekfarm.com.au.

LAKE ARGYLE, ON THE WATER 67/100 □

Swim with freshwater crocodiles in WA's largest man-made freshwater reservoir

This inland sea is a sight for sore eyes, nestled in the Carr Boyd Ranges, a 45-minute drive southeast of Kununurra. By volume, Lake Argyle is Western Australia's largest man-made freshwater reservoir. I can guarantee it's like no other place you've ever seen. Full, the lake covers 980km^2 and holds 10.7 million megalitres of water – enough to fill Sydney Harbour 21 times! More than 25,000 freshwater crocodiles and 26 species of native fish call the lake home, and the islands within the lake are home to various marsupials and reptiles.

Lake Argyle is designated as a RAMSAR Wetland due to the vast number and variety of birds found there. Sometimes, you'll see flocks in the tens of thousands.

01 Service with a smile, with long-term local Greg Smith

02 The lake is said to be home to over 25,000 freshwater crocodiles

The birdwatching doesn't get much better – just ask Greg from Lake Argyle Cruises. Operating for over 26 years, Greg is a long-term local, and he has quite possibly seen every kind of bird that visits the lake or calls it home.

To stand up at Lake Argyle Lookout and gaze upon the lake is one thing, but to really experience Lake Argyle and its islands, you need to get out on the water by boat, paddleboard or kayak. Lake Argyle Cruises rent out a variety of watercraft, or you can join one of its popular cruises in the custom-made vessels, Silver Cobbler II and Yellow Chat, both named after local marine and bird life. I recommend the sunset cruise. Visit lakeargylecruises.com or phone (08) 9168 7687. Bring your swimwear if you can fathom the thought of swimming with 25,000 freshies.

LAKE ARGYLE VILLAGE 68/100 ☐

Cliffside vistas of Australia's most pristine waterway

In 1969 when Lake Argyle was being constructed, a village was set up for workers. These days, this area above the lake is the site for the Lake Argyle Resort and Holiday Park (now owned by the G'day Group after long-term local Charlie Sharpe sold it in 2022) and the nearby Argyle Downs Homestead Museum.

On the drive into Lake Argyle, two minutes before reaching the holiday park, you'll see the turn-off to the Homestead Museum. This is the original home of the pioneering Durack family. They were the first pastoralists to arrive in the east Kimberley in 1883 after their overland cattle drive from Queensland to the Kimberley in a journey that took two years and four months. They settled at Argyle and Ivanhoe Downs. Read about that epic trip in the book Kings In Grass Castles. Stone by stone, the homestead was relocated to its current position from a valley now flooded by the lake's waters. Visitors can drop in and check it out, as it's open daily from April to September.

Just up the road at the Lake Argyle Resort and Holiday Park, you'll find a campground with what is, in my opinion, Australia's most iconic swimming pool. Perched on a hill that looks out across Lake Argyle's northern bays and islands, visitors can enjoy a million-dollar view on a budget. Yep, this sweet infinity pool is part of the caravan park. That means that whether you're staying in a villa or just pitching a tent for the night, you've got access to a swimming pool that you'd expect to find in a five-star resort. While the pool itself isn't huge, the view in front of you is endless! Day visitors can also enjoy the pool for a $10 fee, payable to the office upon arrival.

Lake Argyle Resort is open year-round, but there is nothing better than to watch a massive thunderstorm develop over Lake Argyle from the cool waters of the infinity pool during the build-up from October to December! Access to the lake is possible year-round.

REVOLVER FALLS 69/100 ☐

Western Australia's largest single-drop waterfall

Hidden in the rugged Carr Boyd Ranges on the west side of Lake Argyle, Revolver Falls is the largest single-drop waterfall in the state. This breathtaking, 120m-high plus waterfall only flows during the Wet Season and is spectacular after heavy rains (usually from December to March).

Over the past 25 years, only a small group of experienced hikers have braved extreme Wet Season heat and humidity, plus rocky terrain and sharp spinifex, to take on this challenging 15km hike on foot. There's no set path or trail to follow, so I recommend hiring a local guide if you don't know the area. When I hiked to Revolver in 2017 with my mate Sarel, we got caught in a flash flood near the waterfall's base and thought we would be stuck for days. But fear not; if you'd like to see the falls and are not interested in the hike, you can take a chopper from Kununurra with Helispirit. Visit helispirit.com.au.

Revolver is just one of the thousands of Wet Season waterfalls that appear in the East Kimberley after heavy rainfall (another amazing one close by is Homestead Falls at Lake Argyle). For a landscape photographer, the Wet is a great time to see the Kimberley, but only if you can handle the stifling heat.

GREAT NORTHERN HIGHWAY

Many visitors make it their mission to conquer the thousand kilometres of bitumen between Broome and Kununurra in the fastest time possible. Maybe they'll squeeze in some icons like Purnululu and Geikie Gorge (Danggu), but those that only do that may find the highway to be a long, dreary drive (eye spy another boab, anyone?).

For the discerning traveller, though, this route offers grand opportunities for off-the-beaten-track adventures, unforgettable local Indigenous experiences, and the chance to trace some of the Kimberley's diverse history.

It was roughly this route that Alexander Forrest first charted on his exploration of the area in the late 1870s, changing the course of the Indigenous history, which stretches back thousands and thousands of years. Before Forrest, this was the land exclusively of the Bunuba, Gooniyandi, Jaru and Gija peoples, who never wanted, or needed, gold, cattle or subterranean gas.

Instead, they roamed the flat savannah landscape, dramatic mountain scenery and tropical floodplains, which so characterise the southern part of the Kimberley. For travellers who crave a deep and authentic Kimberley connection, this route, an intersection of Indigenous and western culture, reveals life-changing experiences and profound stories.

Respected Elder, Olive Knight (Kankawa Nagarra), from the community of Wangkatjungka, near Fitzroy Crossing, is a gospel singer-songwriter who has travelled the world with Hugh Jackman.

The most famous of them is likely that of Jandamarra, the Banuba man who, in the late 1800s, staged a guerrilla war against the white police and pastoralists of the area. He gained a legendary reputation for his skill as a tracker and knowledge of the area. Less famous are some of the tragedies of modern colonialism. The Mount King Massacre is told of by many Gija elders around Kununurra and Halls Creek. The Broome vet and bush poet, Dave Morell, captured it in his poem Mount King 1924 (check out Dave's book *Johnny James and Other Verses*). Then, there are stories of gold rushes, incredible feats of pastoralism and epic stock runs that play so richly into the romanticism of the outback and Aussie bush. Take your time, rather than rush, along the Great Northern Highway, and you will hear them all and then some.

While most of the thousand kilometres cut through flat savannah, near Halls Creek the drive becomes particularly dramatic as the highway winds through rugged mountain scenery and wild horses run wild in head-high native grasses. Along the way, you'll have the opportunity to indulge in local art and culture, like at Warmun Art Centre (page 37) and Mimbi Caves, settle in for a hearty pub meal, or explore the histories of the small frontier towns of Halls Creek and Fitzroy Crossing.

Although the highway is sealed, it's wrong to assume this route isn't as interesting as the Gibb River Road. Travelling in a 4WD allows you to side-track at will and discover the best bits of this stretch. So, whether you're casting for a barra in the Fitzroy River, cooling off in the Grotto or testing the acoustics inside Cathedral Gorge, you'll be awestruck and inspired by the many adventures to be had along the Great Northern Highway.

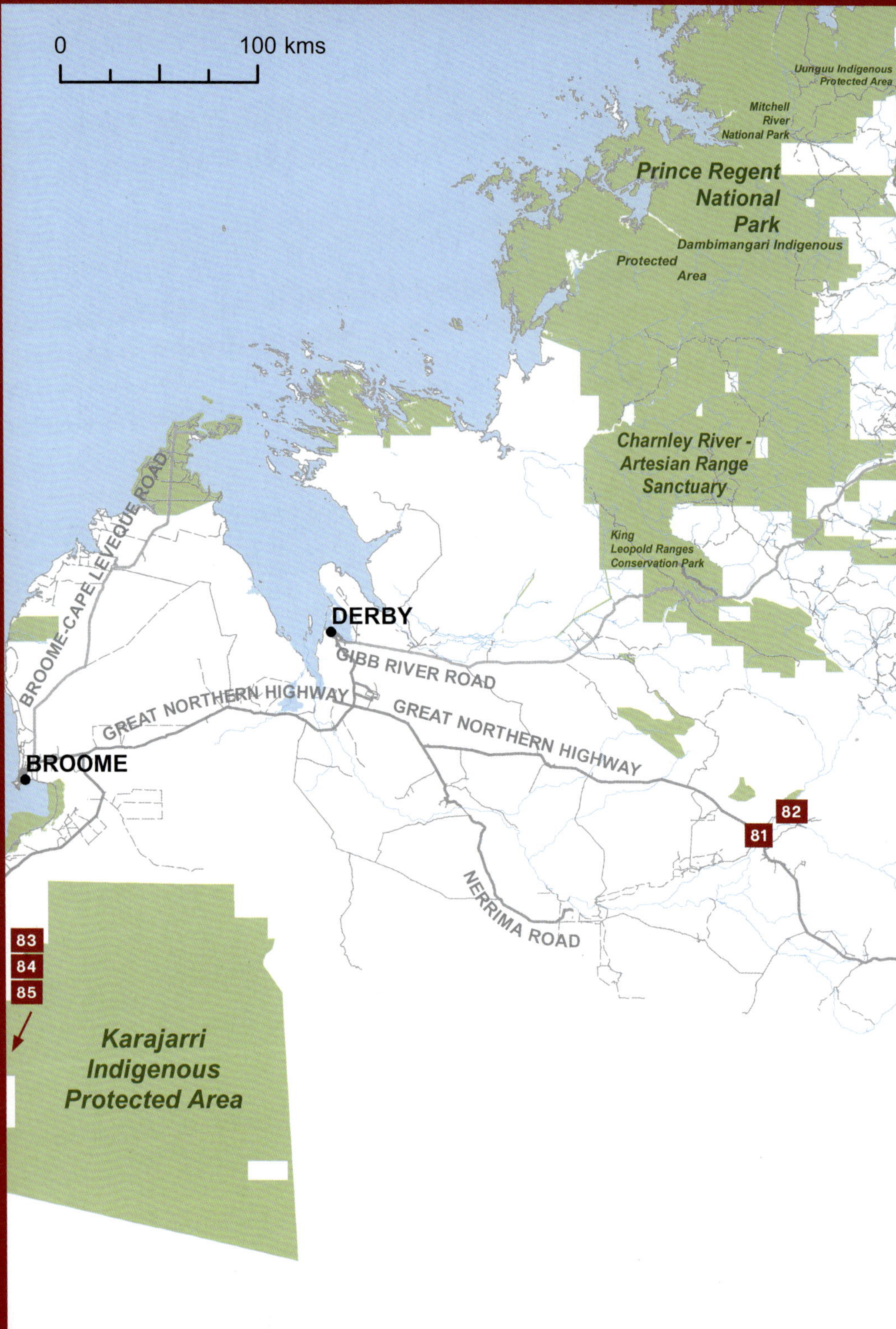

0
100 kms
Uunguu Indigenous Protected Area
Mitchell River National Park
Prince Regent National Park
Dambimangari Indigenous Protected Area
Charnley River - Artesian Range Sanctuary
King Leopold Ranges Conservation Park
DERBY
GIBB RIVER ROAD
BROOME-CAPE LEVEQUE ROAD
GREAT NORTHERN HIGHWAY
GREAT NORTHERN HIGHWAY
BROOME
82
81
NERRIMA ROAD
83
84
85
Karajarri Indigenous Protected Area

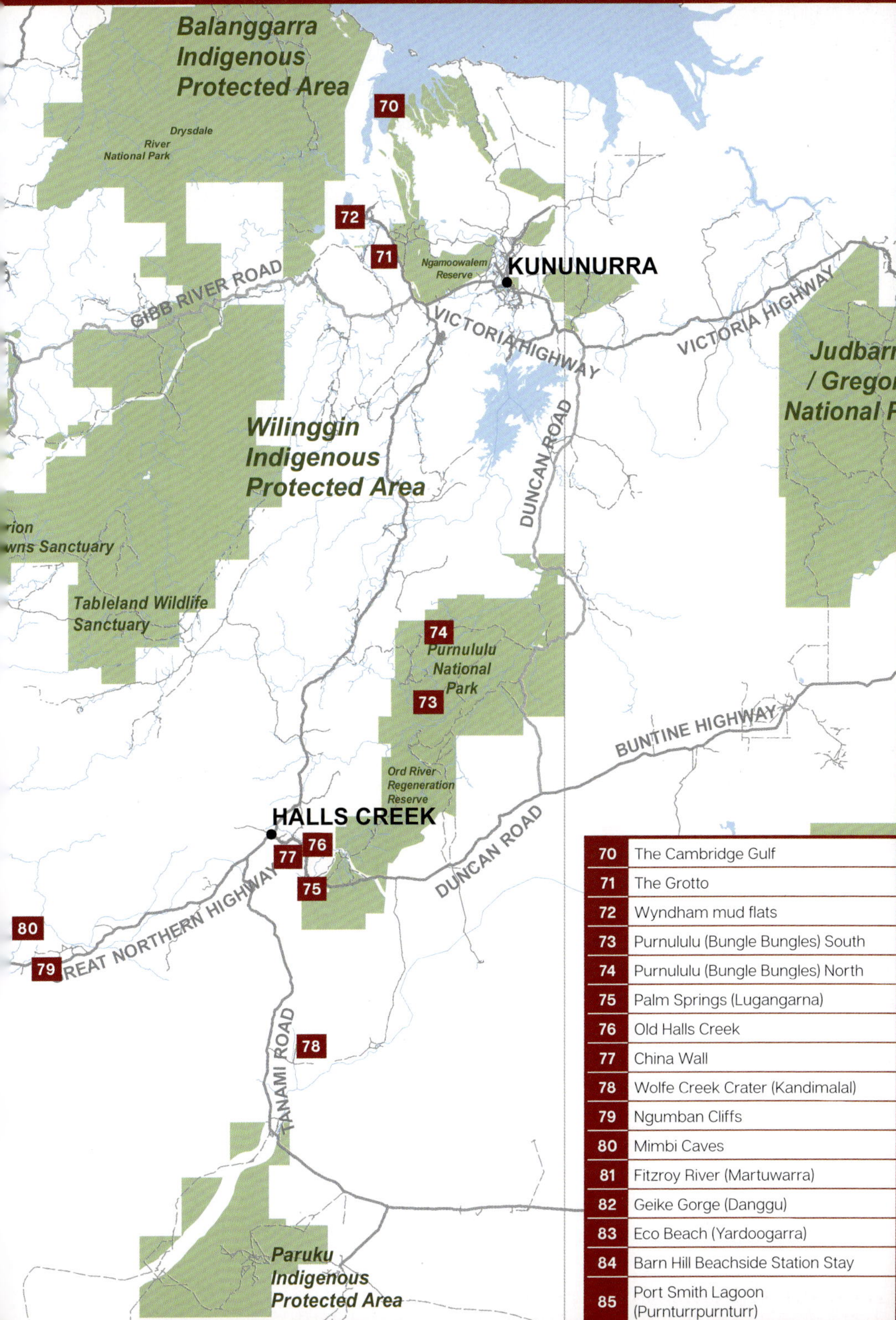

70	The Cambridge Gulf
71	The Grotto
72	Wyndham mud flats
73	Purnululu (Bungle Bungles) South
74	Purnululu (Bungle Bungles) North
75	Palm Springs (Lugangarna)
76	Old Halls Creek
77	China Wall
78	Wolfe Creek Crater (Kandimalal)
79	Ngumban Cliffs
80	Mimbi Caves
81	Fitzroy River (Martuwarra)
82	Geike Gorge (Danggu)
83	Eco Beach (Yardoogarra)
84	Barn Hill Beachside Station Stay
85	Port Smith Lagoon (Purnturrpurnturr)

THE CAMBRIDGE GULF 10/100 ☐

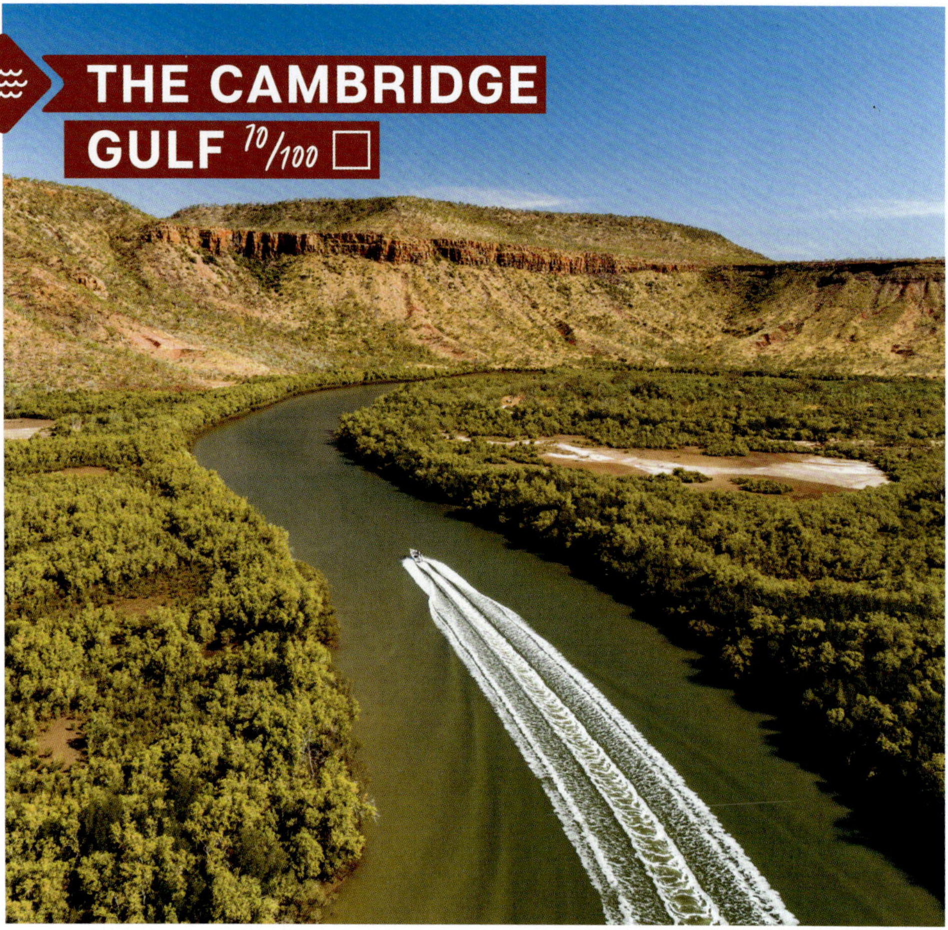

Barra fishing and wild country at the end of the road

The little port town of Wyndham may be the end of the road for those travelling north along the Great Northern Highway, but if you love fishing and spectacular scenery, this is where the adventure begins.

The Cambridge Gulf is renowned amongst circles of die-hard anglers for its incredible barra fishing, especially during the shoulder season months of September to January and the run-off from March to May. With salties aplenty inhabiting these waters and no phone reception, I highly recommend going with a local guide. Brad Pasfield, of East Kimberley Charters, is one of the best. Check eastkimberleycharters.com.au for his current trips on offer.

If you're keen to go fishing without a guide, the King River, which empties into the west arm of the Gulf, has some great barra holes. Turn west just south of Wyndham onto King River Road and try for barra and threadfin salmon off the banks. The river experiences large tides, so check tide times before setting out. Again, keep in mind

the saltwater crocs, the extreme heat and the lack of phone reception. Always tell someone before you go.

Keen to suss the countryside? Upon arrival into Wyndham, the best way to get an overview of the Gulf and the wild, surrounding countryside is to head up the Bastion (Daharwi) Range. 335m above sea level, the Five Rivers Lookout offers spot-on views over the five rivers that run into the Cambridge Gulf - the King, Pentecost, Durack, Ord and Forrest rivers. The views from the lookout are genuinely spectacular, and it's an easy, well-signposted drive out of Wyndham that gets steeper as you go. The lookout is also the location for the annual Stars on the Bastion country music concert, a highlight on the east Kimberley social calendar.

01 The King River, from above, is a sight to behold

02 Lifetime local, Brad Pasfield runs East Kimberley Charters

THE GROTTO 71/100 ☐

140 steps lead down through a gorge to a huge waterhole

With a rope to swing from and a deep pool to float around in, enveloped by sheer gorge walls, the Grotto is a stunning spot. It's one of the best swimming holes between Wyndham and Kununurra and one of the only ones where a 4WD isn't essential. To get there, drive 30km along the sealed Great Northern Highway from Wyndham or 70km from Kununurra and turn off when you see the sign for the Grotto.

A short, flat walk from the carpark leads to a 140-step staircase that spirals steeply into the bottom of the gorge. There's no handrail, so this walk may not be suitable for the elderly or small children.

The waterhole is impressive, and it's estimated the pool is around 100 feet deep. A magnificent waterfall flows into the gorge straight after Wet Season rains, with a second waterfall dropping from the top creek after significant rain. The waterfall disappears during the Dry Season (usually by April, unless there's been late Wet Season rainfall) but the scenery – and a swim – make a stop here worthwhile anytime. Keep an eye out for the small freshwater croc that calls the Grotto home.

WYNDHAM MUD FLATS 72/100 ☐

Watch the landscape transform as your drone puts it into perspective

The topography of Wyndham, Western Australia's northernmost town, is quite interesting, and I always enjoy exploring the mud flats with my drone. As it flies up into the sky, the sheer enormity of the flats becomes apparent; they seem to stretch forever. There are many interesting shapes and patterns, from the tessellations of the cracked mud to the wild rivers that snake their way through the parched earth. The King River and its tributaries can appear to look like giant trees from the sky.

The mud flats have been used in films and photographic campaigns many times. Most famously, in Baz Luhrmann's film *Australia*, King George guides his grandson, Nullah, and a small group across the inhospitable landscape of the Aussie outback.

The mud flats are easy to find. Head 5km south of Wyndham and turn right onto King River Road toward Diggers Rest Station and the Cockburn Range (page 110). You'll see the mud flats spread out before you. The best time is mid-Dry Season onwards, especially to avoid getting bogged from Wet Season rains.

If you continue further along King River Road for 24km, you'll find a giant, old boab tree, reputed to have been used as a prison by police walking groups of Indigenous prisoners to Wyndham. Nearby is Moochalabra Dam, which is Wyndham's water supply. You'll also find artwork in the sandstone overhang and a lovely lily pond, which is a treat to experience.

PURNULULU 73/100 ☐ (BUNGLE BUNGLES) SOUTH

See the famous beehive domes

When the stripey Bungle Bungles were first shown to the world in the 1983 Australian documentary *Wonders of Western Australia*, narrator John Waters described them as "a symphony in stone". Until then, the natural and cultural beauty of Purnululu in the Ord River Valley was known only to the Gija and Jaru custodians, who'd lived here for thousands of years, and to the few pastoralists and stockmen who worked this land. Within five years of that documentary, the Western Australian government created the national park. Within just two decades, it had been granted World Heritage status.

From the Great Northern Highway, it's a 50km rough and corrugated slog along the Spring Creek Track into the national park, and you'll need a 4WD for the journey. Early in the Dry Season, expect to cross a few creeks. Allow at least two hours for the trip. If you're towing a dual axle caravan or trailer, organise to leave it at the Bungle Bungle Caravan Park and continue in unencumbered. Dedicated off-road, single-axle caravans and trailers are permitted if you plan to camp at one of the two campsites within the park - Kurrajong in the north or Walardi in the south.

The famous beehive domes which have captivated the world since the early 1980s are in the southern section of the World Heritage area. Once the floor of an ancient sea, many years of continental drift and erosion from wind and water have formed the iconic domes. The unique tiger stripes are caused by cyanobacteria, a type of algae that creates the dark colour that contrasts beautifully with the rusty, red streaks of oxidised rock. It actually helps preserve the dome-like structures by protecting them from further erosion. Beneath the surface is white sandstone.

The domes are impressive from the ground, and a walk through them is unforgettable. Treat yourself to an early morning or late afternoon chopper flight over the domes for something truly inspiring. Helispirit operates flights inside Purnululu National Park, taking you over the Beehives, Cathedral Gorge, and Piccaninny Gorge. See helispirit.com.au or call 1800 1800 85.

My favourite place in the park is Cathedral Gorge, a stunning natural amphitheatre that you can walk into. It's one of Australia's most striking geological landmarks and a great place to relax. This red-rock gorge was carved out by Wet Season rains that caused whirlpools to swirl and scour within. Get here as early as possible to avoid sharing it with the bus crowds.

If you thought the acoustics in your shower was good, try singing in Cathedral Gorge, or join a tour with Gija guide Bec Sampi at Kingfisher Tours (kingfishertours.com.au), who'll often sing traditional songs, captivating everyone there when she does. Voices carry around the gorge, and you can hear the conversations of people on the other side. The incredible acoustics have drawn various acts, such as the Sydney Symphony Orchestra and world-renowned musicians, to perform special shows over a series of evenings. Magic.

A spectacular walking trail to the gorge sets out from Piccaninny Creek car park, leading you past the striped, beehive-shaped domes that Purnululu National Park is most famous for (4km return).

When the park's access road closes for the Wet Season, scenic flights offer limited opportunities to fly in and see Cathedral Gorge in its monsoon-soaked glory. The rarely-seen waterfall that fills Cathedral Gorge only flows during the Wet. To catch it, book a tour with Helispirit, which has special permission to visit the park when it's closed.

02

01 The dark stripes on the domes are caused by cyanobacteria algae

02 Walking Piccaninny Creek

03 Cathedral Gorge

03

PURNULULU 74/100 ☐ (BUNGLE BUNGLES) NORTH

Watch the chasm's walls light up at midday

All through Purnululu National Park, Indigenous names are the beginnings of ancient stories and culture that's endured despite the pastoral colonisation of the surrounding landscape. In fact, this connection between Indigenous culture and natural phenomena qualified it for UNESCO World Heritage listing. And because Indigenous Australians continued to live largely traditional lifestyles in the region until at least the 1920s, the rich oral history of this part of the Kimberley has been maintained.

It's easy to understand how this landscape affected first Australians' cultural and spiritual identity when you walk through places like Echidna Chasm, which Dreamtime stories say was created when an echidna nosed into a crevice to hide from a cockatoo.

Originally named Mile Deep Chasm by the Wainwrights, who were the first to bring tours into the area, this remarkable chasm that began as a crack in the rock was eroded and widened over time by the power of water and wind. A walk here is one of the best things to do in the national park, and you'll feel a sense of peace wash over you as you explore this unique gorge. Some parts are only shoulder-width apart but tower to almost 180 metres!

As you enter past a stand of cabbage tree palms, you will feel the cool air rushing past. If you stop and gaze skyward, you can see more of the Livistona palms waving about from 180m up on the conglomerate boulders. When the sun lines up directly above the gorge around midday, its walls ignite with the most incredible shades of rich red and rusty orange.

It's an easy to moderate 1.4km-return walk into the gorge, setting out from the Echidna Chasm car park 19km north of the visitor centre. A reasonable level of agility is required when climbing the steel ladder section at the end. Don't miss the walk to Osmand Lookout from the Echidna Chasm carpark for fantastic views over the stunning Osmand Range.

There's more to learn along the three longer walks, which all begin at the Bloodwoods carpark, with the Mini Palms walk a local favourite. On the 4.2km return trek, you'll wander through a natural amphitheatre of rich red rock into a lost world of palms and lush vegetation.

The best place to finish the day is Kungkalanayi Lookout, just north of the Spring Creek Track junction. Sitting high on the plains, it offers a 360° view of the surrounding country. It's spectacular late in the day as the landscape changes colours under the setting sun. Set up camp at Kurrajong campsite if you're staying overnight – here, the natural darkness and lack of light pollution (and mobile phone glare) allow for an incredible star show.

01 The entrance to Echidna Chasm illuminates when the midday sun shines directly overhead

PALM SPRINGS (LUGANGARNA) 75/100 ☐

Year-round swimming in a freshwater spring and free camping

In the desert country surrounding Halls Creek, swimming spots are like discovering gold, which is why this oasis is worthy of the 40km mission from Halls Creek down the dusty, unsealed Duncan Road. Due to the rough track, a 4WD is recommended, and it's also worth checking current road conditions with the Halls Creek Visitor Centre – phone (08) 9168 6262.

Known as Lugangarna in the local Jaru language, Palm Springs is a permanent freshwater swimming hole on the Black Elvire River. Because it's spring-fed, you can swim here year-round, unlike at the nearby Sawpit Gorge, which dries up after the Wet Season's rains. Palm Springs is a popular spot for locals to picnic, and it's also home to various birds, fish and some shy freshwater crocs. Fringing the water's edge are some date palms believed to have been planted by Afghan cameleers who passed through the region in the 1800s.

Camping here is a great way to enjoy the spot and take another swim in the morning. There's a small area (near the road) for free 24-hour camping, an excellent location to set up for the night.

OLD HALLS CREEK 16/100 ☐

The site of WA's first gold rush

On the drive to Palm Springs, about 13km from Halls Creek on the unsealed Duncan Road, you'll find Old Halls Creek. This is the site of Western Australia's first gold discovery when a prospector named Charlie Hall found gold in 1885. Some say he found a whopping 28-ounce nugget (almost 1kg). However, the fact is that he only presented 10 ounces of small nuggets when he arrived at Derby, so it's hard to say if there's any truth to the legend.

Either way, Hall and his friends' discovery of alluvial gold triggered a gold rush of thousands of men to the region. Some of them remain today in the old cemetery. Other ruins include a few street signs and old mud-brick buildings, including the original post office.

This is also the location where the Royal Flying Doctor service was born. Jimmy Darcy, a young and very capable stockman, was operated on by the postmaster (after suffering a nasty fall from his horse) whilst waiting for a doctor to arrive by ship and an overland expedition. Unfortunately, he passed away a day before the doctor arrived, making John Flynn more eager to assist those living remotely with sufficient medical support. flyingdoctor.org.au

If you visit after Wet Season rain, head to the nearby Caroline Pool (or Wimirri in the Jaru language). Here you'll find sandy banks around the seasonal waterhole (pictured above) and some nice shady bushwalking. Five minutes' drive northwest from Old Halls Creek via a sometimes heavily corrugated road, this is also a free camping area (24 hours maximum) with a drop toilet. Take all rubbish with you.

STAY

While the main townsites of Fitzroy Crossing and Halls Creek have hotels and campgrounds with restaurant and pool facilities, the real gems are found down the various 4WD tracks that lead off the highway.

The evenings are pure magic out here, and the mid-Dry Season's freezing night-time temperatures are worth it to fall asleep to the sounds of the Aussie bush and the twinkling of a million stars.

BUNGLE BUNGLES SAVANNAH LODGE

If you really want to immerse yourself in all the Bungles have to offer, the locally-owned Savannah Lodge, in the southern section of the park, is the place to base yourself. Stay in one of the 26 stand-alone, hard-walled cabins and cool off in the pool (yep, there's a pool) or with a drink and a meal at the restaurant. Book at bunglebunglesavanahlodge.com.au.

FITZROY RIVER LODGE

Whether you've got your own accommodation or prefer the comfort of solid walls around you, the Lodge is the top spot in Fitzroy Crossing to stay while you explore. Choose from powered or unpowered camping on a grassy lawn, safari tents, studios, and motel rooms. There's a nice swimming pool ti cool off in and the onsite restaurant is pretty good, too. fitzroyriverlodge.com.au.

CAMPING WITH CUSTODIANS

Want to camp in the best locations while giving money directly to local Indigenous communities? The Camping with Custodians initiative is where it's at. Check out Jarlarloo Riwi Mimbi Campground at Mimbi Caves (pictured above) and Violet Valley Campground (Purnululu/ Bungle Bungles community) at waitoc.com.au. Ted Hall of Luridgii Tours also offers camping at Second Gorge for those joining his 4WD tagalong tours. Read more at luridgiitours.com.au.

CHINA WALL 77/100 ☐

A wall of quartz pushed up from the earth's surface

The unique rock formation known as China Wall is 7km south of Halls Creek along Duncan Road. Rising 6m in some parts and stretching several kilometres across the rugged landscape, the quartz vein is amazingly resistant to weathering and looks almost man-made. At sunset, the whole landscape lights up, and the white quartz of the rock formation glows as dusk settles over the hills.

While it may not compare to the grandeur of its Chinese namesake, what's amazing about this wall is that it's a natural feature carved by the wind and rain. It's known as Burraluba in the Jaru language and Mulugunjiny in Kija. The rocky outcrop is on private land, so close the gate behind you when you enter and leave.

Following Duncan Road further east will take you to Caroline Pool, a semi-permanent freshwater swimming hole (it's often pretty small by the end of the Dry Season) with a 24-hour free campsite. See page 179.

WOLFE CREEK CRATER (KANDIMALAL)

78/100 ☐

Outback sensory overload plus free camping

Wolfe Creek Crater's 875m diameter makes it the world's second-biggest rimmed crater and certainly one of the best-preserved (arid Australia has a heap of great craters because they don't get eroded by flooding rivers and water catchments). Scientists have found meteorite fragments up to 4km away!

Known as Kandimalal to the desert peoples who tell stories of its creation, it has tremendous wow-factor, amplified by its near-perfect circular shape, lack of erosion and its crash site on the flat plains of the Australian outback.

Europeans first encountered the crater in 1947 when geologists observed it during an aerial survey. Yet, strangely, it is still relatively unknown, although the release of the fictional, outback horror film 'Wolf Creek' (spelt without the 'e') in 2005 brought it to the attention of the wider public.

The crater is located on the edge of the Tanami Desert, about 145km south of Halls Creek via a sometimes very heavily

corrugated road. Take the signposted turn off the Great Northern Highway, 18km west of Halls Creek.

There's a free, national park campground 400m from the crater, with cleared sites and pit toilets (BYO water and take all rubbish away with you). You've travelled all the way out here; why not stay for the night and watch the sunset over the crater, then a blanket of stars appear.

At the crater, you can do a 200m walk up to the rim, then continue around its circumference. Hikers heading to the middle of the impact site have also worn a track to the bottom. I love getting up early to hike to the rim at sunrise during the Dry Season (when temperatures can drop below zero at night – come prepared). It's amazing to just stand and imagine the moment when the 50,000-tonne meteorite travelling at 15km per second crashed into the earth.

The road can be inaccessible during the Wet. You can view the crater by air on a scenic flight from Halls Creek. Visit northwestregionalair.com.au for more information.

NGUMBAN CLIFFS 79/100 ☐

A wild west vista south, toward the Great Sandy Desert

Ten minutes' drive east from Mimbi Caves along the Great Northern Highway is Ngumban Cliffs, an essential break for everyone driving this route. Exiting the highway, the road winds up a hill to a lookout perched on the side of a gorge, with sweeping views over the Mueller Ranges.

The red soil contrasts nicely with the spinifex grasses and dramatic scenery, making for an awesome photo, especially at sunset when the countryside glows. You can free camp for up to 24 hours and there are toilets, picnic tables and BBQs, plus a dump point. As this is unfenced cattle country, you're best to sleep the night here if you're driving through in the late afternoon, anyway.

A morning walk in this terrain inspires thoughts about the traditional way of life for the Aboriginal peoples who've called this place home for thousands of years. In remote places like this, it can be hard to comprehend where food, water and shelter might be found. But, the more you learn about this terrain, the more you'll realise that all of these things are within walking distance and ancient songlines lead people to find out an abundance of resources in this environment.

There is a spring nearby called the Ngumban Spring (or Pinnacle Spring), which is a source of freshwater. There is also an abundance of bush tucker found in the area including Konkerberry, boab nuts, bush banana, bush tomatoes, yams, bush turkeys, goanna and black bream.

MIMBI CAVES 80/100 ☐

Caves, culture, and a shmick campground

Take an Indiana Jones-style adventure deep into the heart of Gooniyandi country at Mimbi Caves, an ancient Devonian reef and one of Western Australia's largest cave systems. It runs all the way to Danggu and Windjana Gorges in the western Kimberley.

90km east of Fitzroy Crossing and only 3.4km off the highway via Mt. Pierre Station's gravel road, Mimbi (meaning 'cave') is 100 per cent owned and operated by the Gooniyandi people.

To see the caves, it's best to join a guide from Girloorloo Tours. They will welcome you with a muntha (smoking ceremony) before walking you through narrow gaps and large caverns of the caves, feeding you up with tasty damper and bush tucker and sharing their Dreaming story of the blue-tongue lizard and the mudlark. In the story, the lizard tries to save her babies from floodwaters by asking a reluctant mudlark to keep them safe in her nest. The mudlark refused, so the lizard and her babies were swept away in the floodwater.

The Gooniyandi believe that the blue-tongue created the landscape around Mimbi Caves. During your torchlight tour, you'll see Indigenous rock art paintings, petroglyphs (engravings) and marine fossils from the Devonian era. In fact, it's believed that Mimbi is one of the world's most significant Devonian fossil sites.

It really is impressive to see an ancient barrier reef so far inland and surrounded by desert country! The tour may also offer an opportunity for a cool dip in one of Mimbi's permanent freshwater pools, a 'refreshing' treat worthy of stripping off for, if only to quickly jump in and out.

At the nearby Jarlarloo Riwi campground, there are scattered campsites, hot showers and a BBQ shelter. Remember to bring your warm woollies – evening temperatures can drop to freezing during the Dry Season. Staying at the campsite is convenient if you plan to join the 8 am cave tour (Monday to Saturday - meet at the cave entrance). Otherwise, there's a 2 pm cave tour from Monday to Thursday. Visit mimbicaves.com.au for campground and tour bookings or phone 0437 546 873 or 0477 355 671.

FITZROY RIVER (MARTUWARRA) 81/100 □

A mighty river that becomes a raging torrent during the Wet

The Fitzroy – known as Mardoowarra or Martuwarra in Nyikina or Bandaralngarri in Banuba Indigenous peoples – is one of the Kimberley's most significant rivers. It rises from Wunaamin Miliwundi (formerly King Leopold) and Mueller ranges in the central region. It flows for over 700km west, then north, into King Sound, south of Derby. Because the catchment is so large (nearly 94,000km^2), an incredible amount of water flows downstream during the Wet Season; enough, some say, to fill Sydney Harbour in under eight hours. During the January 2023 floods (which stranded my family and I in Broome), as much water flowed down it in one day as Perth uses in 20 years!

Over the Dry Season, as it gradually dries up, deeper pools buoyed by groundwater reserves create permanent refuges for a myriad of endemic and endangered species, not to mention concentrated barramundi holes. The fishing can be all-time. It's one of Australia's last truly wild rivers in pristine health. Given its size and abundance, it's little surprise the river is exceptionally important to aboriginal people who've grown up around it and the aquatic and bird species that depend on it for survival.

The Western Australian government had talked of damming the river for use in mining and agricultural irrigation schemes, pulling billions of litres of water from the environment and endangering the rare freshwater sawfish that call it home; however, intense campaigning against the idea has so far ensured the plans have not come to fruition. Find out more at likenowhereelse.org.au.

The Fitzroy and its 20 tributaries provide fantastic fishing, especially for bream, barramundi and cherabin, and you could probably spend a lifetime exploring them. If you don't have that long, start at Camballin Caravan Park, the riverside camp on Looma Station, still little-known in the Kimberley. Phone 0499 903 314. Remember to be croc-wise at all times, as salties inhabit the river's lower reaches.

GEIKIE GORGE 82/100 □ (DANGGU)

An amazing gorge carved through an ancient limestone reef

Known as Danggu (pronounced darn-goo) to the Bunuba people, this stunning chasm in Geikie Gorge National Park is loved by photographers for its dramatic, bleached limestone walls. The striking colour is thanks to the Fitzroy River's tremendous Wet Season floods that raise the water level in Geikie Gorge to dramatic heights.

Located in the heart of Bunuba country, 20km from Fitzroy Crossing, the gorge is part of an ancient limestone barrier reef that flourished in the Devonian period. Today it's home to freshwater crocs, rock wallabies, stingrays, barramundi and the rare freshwater Leichhardt's sawfish.

The best way to experience the gorge is on a one-hour boat cruise, which operates between May and October aboard the vessel *Ms Casey Ross* (named after a late Elder). Book with Fitzroy Crossing's Visitor Centre, phone (08) 9191 5355, or online through bunuba.com (up to four tours run a day). This website also offers information on the four walking trails, including details of their cultural significance. For example, the 1.2 km Bun.gu trail, which was an important meeting place for ceremonies and trading for tens of thousands of years for the Bunuba and Gooniyandi peoples.

EAT

Lonely outback highways were once characterised by their limited and often unhealthy food options (day-old, bain-marie dim sims, anyone?), but there are some decent food options along the Highway, even for those with specific dietary needs or those who just crave a great coffee.

The ones mentioned below offer fantastic food in surprising locations (surprising, considering how remote each of the three are). Remote can also often mean short-staffed, so, if your food is taking a while, relax and have a yarn with fellow travellers. Most folks have a good story to tell, out here!

CROC CAFE AND BAKERY

Ever wondered what a crocodile pie taste like? Or, a barramundi pie? Well, this is the place to give it a try! Wyndham's Croc Cafe and Bakery is a local favourite; it's family-run and offers a cabinet full of pastries and other tummy-fillers, including fresh bread and fresh salad rolls. There's a shady courtyard out the back, otherwise take your tucker up to the top of the Five Rivers Lookout (page 171) for awesome vistas of the surrounding countryside.

WILLAIRE BRIDGE ROADHOUSE

With its memorable timber signs pointing out the distances to each major town east to west and proving how far you are from anything, the food here is spot on, thanks to Neralie and her team. Eggs benny at brekky is the perfect way to start a big day, while the evening service often includes live music. Camping is offered out back, too. Visit willareroadhouse.com.

BIANCAVILLA PIZZA

Take a culinary journey to Sicily without leaving the Kimberley. Sicilian pizza chef Benedetto Sardina serves delicious and authentic pizzas each night at Barn Hill Station at Biancavilla Pizza. The prices are also quite reasonable, from $22 for a Margherita or $27 for Benny's Special. As Benny would say, 'in crust we trust!' See the current menu at facebook.com/biancavillapizza.

ECO BEACH 83/100 ☐ (YARDOOGARRA)

Luxe, beachside glamping.

When Tropical Cyclone Rosita battered the Kimberley coast in April 2000, Eco Beach copped the full force of winds that topped 290km/h. Undeterred, the resort's visionary – local builder Karl Plunkett – rebuilt it from scratch and reopened it nine years later in 2009.

It's since changed hands a few times. These days, Eco's accommodation comprises 25 solar-powered villas and 30 safari glamping tents nestled in the coastal bushland. Priced from $225 per night for a garden tent ($495 if you want an ocean glimpse). If you come in the shoulder season, check its website, as it's been known to advertise special offers when bookings are low. ecobeach.com.au.

There's plenty to do, but relaxation and connecting with nature are the name of the game here. For sunset, the best location is the infinity-edged pool. The hammocks down on the beach are also a great option for daytime 'chillaxing'. Take a book and tune out. Walking Country with Traditional Owner Neil McKenzie or fishing from Little Yardi Creek for threadfin salmon and mangrove jack are some tour options, if you want to splash some cash.

If you're not staying at Eco, you can still visit as a day tripper (a good option if you're camping at the nearby Barn Hill, page 190). The Broome catamaran *Karma IV*, operated by an old schoolmate, Chaz Kennedy, also runs day cruises down to Eco Beach from Broome. Budget $199 per person for a 9-hour day, including lunch at Jack's Bar in Eco Beach. Cruises depart from Gantheaume Point. karma4.com.au.

BARN HILL BEACHSIDE STATION STAY 84/100 ☐

Dog-friendly camping, pizzas and a bowling green.

The same campervans return to Barn Hill year after year, and it's easy to see why. Perched on top of red cliffs, looking out over the sea, this rustic, dog-friendly station stay has a family vibe and plenty to do. Rustic is the key word here, but, in my opinion, the open-roofed outdoor showers are part of what makes it unique.

Turning off the Great Northern Highway just 9km south of Eco Beach, you'll find yourself bumping along 10km of a sandy track on Thangoo Station, one of the Kimberley's few family-owned beef cattle stations. There aren't many signs of it being a cattle station, though, apart from the three gates that you need to open and close on your way in.

The camping is divided into unpowered in the dirt ($35 standard site, $45 oceanview) or 6amp powered with grass and shade

(from $45). The oceanview unpowered sites are the better option for incredible, sweeping vistas down to the sea. Arrive just after campers start checking out at 10 am to get your spot, as the oceanview sites are in hot demand. Check-in isn't officially until 1 pm, so you'll need to wait a bit, but once people get a prime spot, they may not be leaving for a while. The community vibe and activities at this campsite are strong, and you may stay longer than expected. If you're after a bit more space and privacy, the $80-a-night timber beach shelters are a worthy upgrade.

One of the unique quirks of Barn Hill is the bowling green, right near the office and food area. There are competitions three times a week. Each Saturday, there's a band, and every Wednesday, there's a communal BBQ. But the star of the show is the pizzas, cooked up by Sicilian pizza chef Benedetto Sardina.

PORT SMITH LAGOON (PURNTURRPURNTURR)

85/100 ☐

Fishing, camping and a lagoon

If you're travelling from the south, Port Smith may be your first experience of the Kimberley, sitting about 160km by road south of Broome and 25 minutes off the highway. Its charm lies in the simple, red-dirt caravan park and endless days spent exploring the white sandy beaches of the surrounding estuaries. Think turquoise lagoons, spectacular sunsets, and awesome fishing.

Nestled in Karajarri country, just north of Western Australia's largest remote Aboriginal community Bidyadanga, Port Smith has been a fishing destination for

decades, known for the world-class angling and the tidal estuary filled with mud crabs. If you bring a boat, you can launch it from the beach to explore the maze of creeks in the area. Remember, tides in the area can exceed 9 metres. If you park your 4WD and go off fishing, make sure it's parked above the high tide line. Not everyone does...

Expect good catches of bluebone, snapper, trevally, queenies and maybe even some barra. In the lagoon, you have a good chance of catching sand whiting and bream from the sand. When the tide goes out, if you wander amongst the deeper pools of water left behind, you might find turtles and other fish awaiting higher water and their escape.

Run by the Traditional Custodians, the park and surrounding country have seen some recent investments into infrastructure and environmental initiatives, making some of the non-fishing attractions easier to access. You'll need to organise a permit to visit some of the surrounding areas, but it's good value at just $15 a day. Order it at ktla.org.au.

Through whale watching season, head north along the winding sand tracks to Mirntanymartaji - Gourdan Bay, where pearling camps replaced the traditional fishing grounds. There's a great walk southeast along the seacliffs to Indigenous fish traps. You might see whales congregating in the sheltered waters or turtles swimming below. Detour to Tarkataarkangurru – Saddle Hill Cliffs for epic sunset picnics above the pindan red cliffs and oche sand beaches.

South of the caravan park, Cowrie Creek is a popular, land-based fishing spot, where with a bit of exploration, you can find a decent mangrove hole full of fish or crabs to take back to camp for dinner. A near-shore reef is just off the beach, where you can park your 4WD to hang out for the day and enjoy the excellent swimming.

Currently, the only camping is allowed at the Port Smith Lagoon Caravan Park, which has some cabins, 100 powered sites and an unpowered overflow area for when the main section fills up. Expect to be camping on red dirt but amongst improving facilities and in company of plenty of midgies (bring repellent).

THE KIMBERLEY COAST

Waterfalls, coastal gorges, islands and fishing – the Kimberley coast is simply spectacular, stretching its way north and east from Broome all the way to the Northern Territory border.

Part of the beauty of this coastline is how amazingly underdeveloped it is. For the sheer size of it and the variety of activities on offer, it's incredible that so few people know about it. I remember my school days in Broome when my dad, Bruce, joined a trip on the original *Kimberley Quest*. Owning a travel agency, my folks had travelled all around the world, yet dad raved about the Kimberley coast, saying it was the best trip he'd ever taken. Once he got back, he and mum set up the Kimberley Cruise Centre, a travel agency selling cruises aboard the boats cruising north of Broome (there were about three boats back then, but now there are two dozen). After school, I went on to work as a deckie for a few of them.

As I learned from my travels, the coastline is littered with amazing spots, and it would be easy to write a whole book about them. Len Zell has done a great job with his book *Kimberley Coast*. I dare say that not much has changed since it was published in 2007. In the following pages, I've chosen some of the coast's prettiest waterfalls, unique tidal phenomena and a couple of reefs out on the continental shelf, well away from the crocs (for the divers and surfers amongst us).

These places are so remote there are no roads to any of them. The best, and almost only, way to visit is by private boat or cruise, of which there are regular departures from March to October, departing Broome, Wyndham and Darwin.

The first question everyone naturally asks is, "When's the best time to come?" March, April, September and October are the shoulder season, and the barra are on the bite, but the weather is unbearably hot for most people. For thundering waterfalls, straight after the Wet Season is best. Most waterfalls (except for the few spring-fed ones) usually turn to a trickle by late May, before completely drying up. Humpback whales are everywhere from July to October. Mid-year is the most popular time, when travellers escape winter down south. But really, any time is good if you want to see glorious gorges, explore empty beaches, have fun fishing and experience starry nights and undeveloped wilderness that is so hard to find these days.

Naturally, I recommend you call my oldies to book your Kimberley cruise. They have, after all, been in the game for over two decades, and they've travelled aboard most of the boats (yep, tough job, but someone's gotta do it). Chat with Bruce or Terri on 1800 677 830 or see kimberleycruises.com. Tell 'em I sent ya!

0
100 kms
100
93
95
Prince Rege
Nation
Pa
92
Dambimangari
Indigenous
Protected Area
90
91
89
86
87
88
Charnley River -
Artesian Range
Sanctuary
Bardi Jawi
Indigenous
Protected Area
King
Leopold Ranges
Conservation Park
BROOME-CAPE LEVEQUE ROAD
DERBY
GIBB RIVER ROAD
GREAT NORTHERN HIGHWAY
99
BROOME
GREAT NORTHERN HIGHWAY

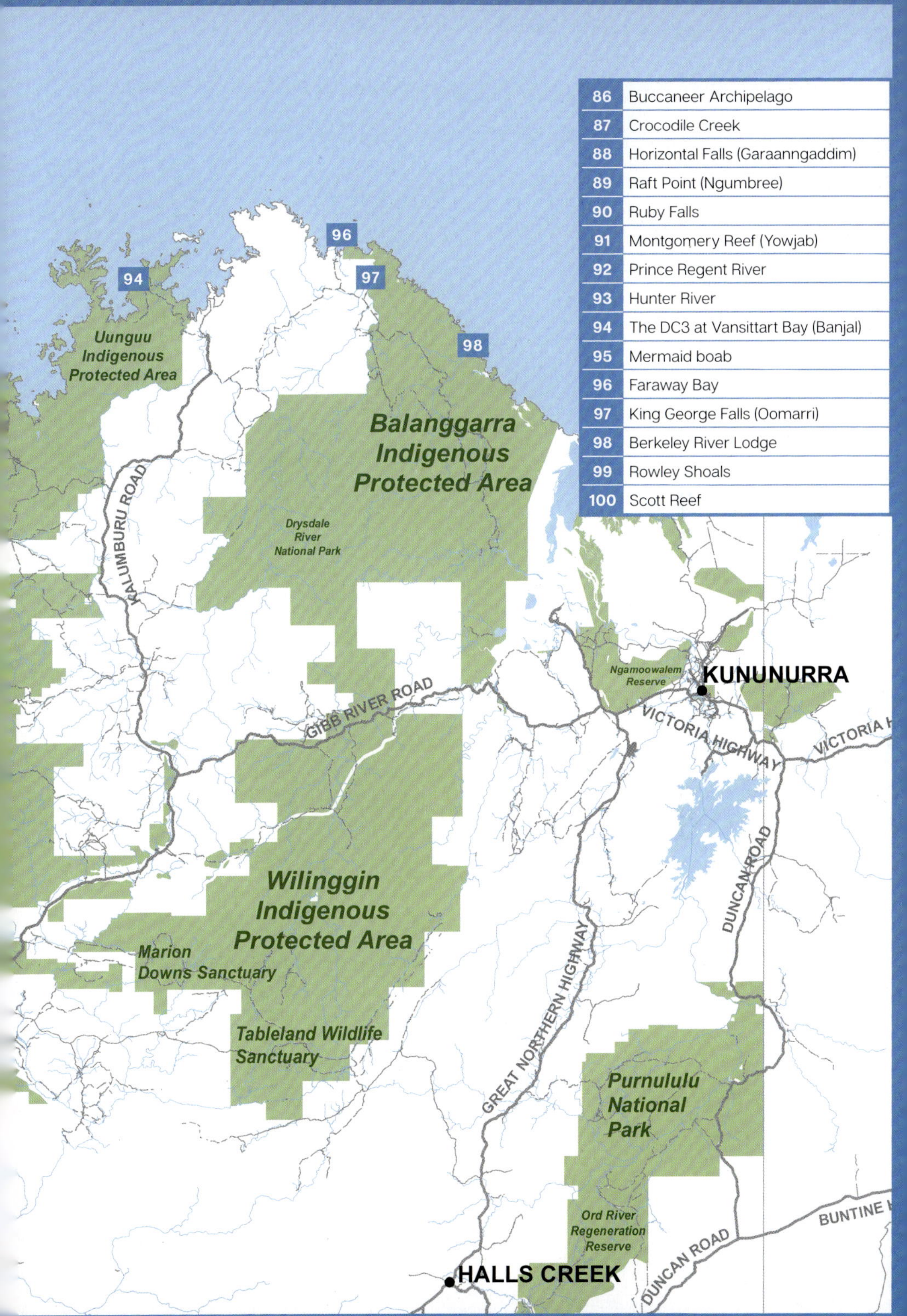
86 Buccaneer Archipelago
87 Crocodile Creek
88 Horizontal Falls (Garaanngaddim)
89 Raft Point (Ngumbree)
90 Ruby Falls
91 Montgomery Reef (Yowjab)
92 Prince Regent River
93 Hunter River
94 The DC3 at Vansittart Bay (Banjal)
95 Mermaid boab
96 Faraway Bay
97 King George Falls (Oomarri)
98 Berkeley River Lodge
99 Rowley Shoals
100 Scott Reef
94
96
97
98
Uunguu Indigenous Protected Area
Balanggarra Indigenous Protected Area
Drysdale River National Park
KALUMBURU ROAD
GIBB RIVER ROAD
Ngamoowalem Reserve
KUNUNURRA
VICTORIA HIGHWAY
DUNCAN ROAD
Wilinggin Indigenous Protected Area
Marion Downs Sanctuary
Tableland Wildlife Sanctuary
GREAT NORTHERN HIGHWAY
Purnululu National Park
Ord River Regeneration Reserve
HALLS CREEK
BUNTINE

BUCCANEER 86/100 □ ARCHIPELAGO

A thousand islands inhabited only by wildlife

The Buccaneer Archipelago is a group of around 1,000 islands located along the Kimberley coast, north of Derby. These remote and largely uninhabited islands are known for their rugged terrain and pristine, white sandy beaches that few have ever set foot upon.

Captain Phillip Parker King named the Buccaneer Archipelago commemorating William Dampier's 1688 visit. Dampier was little better than a pirate, but he was the first to circumnavigate the world three times and was the first Englishman to visit Australia. Of course, Indigenous Australians have inhabited this region for thousands of years. Their rock art, found on islands and across the mainland, dates to the last ice age.

The tides and whirlpools in the archipelago can be treacherous for sailors, as evidenced by graves on some islands. These tides are the largest in the tropics, creating one of the world's greatest natural wonders, the Horizontal Falls.

If you are cruising the archipelago in a boat or sailing vessel, it might be tempting to jump overboard for a swim in the beautiful turquoise sea, but the presence of salties means this isn't a good idea in most places. Instead, head to Silica Beach on Hidden Island. This 150m long beach has the whitest, squeakiest sand you'll ever come across, as the water catchment behind it is made up of very rare, almost pure silica quartzite with no other minerals to colour the sand. You can swim safely here, provided you set someone up on the rocky outcrop that's an ideal croc-watching lookout. Deep water makes it possible to moor quite close to the beach, allowing vessels to make a quick stopover while exploring the archipelago.

Commercially operating Kimberley cruises run from March to October. If you don't have time for a cruise, take a scenic flight from Broome or Derby. Light aircraft fly over the islands on day tours, and visitor centres in Broome or Derby can get you on board.

CROCODILE CREEK 87/100 ☐

A cascading waterfall with a spring-fed billabong above

In the traditional country of the Dambeemangarddee people, Crocodile Creek spills into the ocean at one of the most visited waterfalls on the Kimberley coast (all 22 commercial cruise operators, plus private yachties, stop in here). It's found on an isolated stretch of the mainland, south of Cockatoo Island and accessible only by boat. Despite the name, it's a popular swimming hole for passing yachties and commercial cruise operators.

During spring high tides, the sea flows right into the pool, mingling with the freshwater that cascades over the falls. These high tides allow crocs to access the lower pool, though, so play it safe and climb carefully up the gradually inclining sandstone walls to reach the lovely, pandanus-fringed billabong at the top of the falls. Safe from salties, the spring-fed pool provides a pretty view over the waterfall.

At high tide, boats can motor straight up to the rock bar for the short walk to the lower pool. As the tide drops, a ladder is exposed that makes access easier.

HORIZONTAL FALLS (GARAANNGADDIM) 88/100 ☐

Ride the rapids as tidal waters gush through narrow coastal gorges

When I got my driver's license as a teenager in Broome, my first job was driving a bus full of tourists to Derby, where they'd jump onto a seaplane and fly to Horizontal Falls. The seaplane would set course for Talbot Bay in the McLarty Ranges, landing close to the two gaps in the landscape. There, a boat would take guests on a thrilling ride as the tide rushes through the distinct horizontal 'waterfall'. There are two gaps; one is 12 metres wide, and the other is 20. The smaller gap is now closed to tourist boats, as it is simply too dangerous to pass through. However, tour boats still go through the bigger one (despite a few accidents in recent years).

You may prefer to use the indigenous name, if you can pronounce it – Garaanngaddim, in the language of the Dambeemangarddee people. With the Department of Parks and Wildlife, they jointly manage the area, which is part of the Lalang-garram / Horizontal Falls Marine Park.

I'm not sure who came up with the name, but the idea of a waterfall that flows horizontally can cetainly be confusing. (Potentially, it was the staff from Paspaley's pearl farm nearby). When thinking of a waterfall, it almost always conjures up an image of water tumbling down over a rocky ledge. Therefore, a horizontal ocean waterfall may be difficult to imagine. At Horizontal Falls, huge tides force water so quickly through extremely narrow gorges that it banks up on one side, creating a surging white rapid. Passing over the falls in a boat, you can experience the change in sea level. The bigger the tide, the more exhilarating the ride!

When the tide changes, the waterfall reverses. It's an impressive scene from the sky, but it's best to ride the rapids with an experienced Kimberley skipper to feel the power of the falls. Book your trip during a full or new moon when big spring and king tides surge through the gorge. Call the team at the visitor centre in Broome, (08) 9195 2200, or in Derby, (08) 9191 1426.

RAFT POINT (NGUMBREE)

A stunning coastal scarp with awesome views and rock art

Raft Point is an imposing bluff rising from the middle of Doubtful Bay in the heart of Worrorra country. With a seemingly harsh living environment, it may be hard to imagine, but Indigenous peoples once used this beach as a launch site for fishing trips, riding the tides in mangrove-wood rafts using paddles only for steering. Early explorers to the region saw their double-layered rafts on the beach here.

For sweeping coastal vistas over neighbouring Steep Island, climb 150m above the beach to reach a sandstone overhang. Here you'll find Ngumbree art gallery, a series of rock canvases crowded with the ochre art of the Wandjina, the creator spirit of the Worrorra, Ngarinyin and Wumumbul peoples. With large, round eyes and halos around their heads, Wandjinas are associated with rain and seasonal regeneration (see page 39).

Their location, high on the bluff, really evokes wonder about the amazing resourcefulness of the Indigenous people who have lived and thrived off this remote country for thousands of years. Local Elders say the paintings have been continually maintained for the last 5,000 years, possibly longer.

Like much of this coastline, Raft Point is only accessible by boat, and plenty of commercial cruise boats stop by from March to October.

RUBY FALLS 90/100 □

An amazing waterfall with a hidden spa pool above

Testament to how untamed and still unexplored the Kimberley is, Ruby Falls was only discovered by the modern tourism operators in the past 30 years. Chris 'Trippy' Tucker (who owns the Great Escape Charter Company), named it after his daughter. Now it's a popular inclusion on cruise itineraries, and with gorgeous freshwater rock pools, it's easy to see why.

Access to the falls is via the eastern arm of Red Cone Creek, in the southeast corner of Doubtful Bay. Because seawater floods the bottom pool on spring and king tides, it's better to climb above the falls for croc-free swimming. After clambering up the rocky cliffs to the left of the falls (climb slowly and carefully, as the rocks can be slippery), you'll discover a lovely natural spa pool beneath a small waterfall and a gorgeous vista over the main pool below. Further exploration upstream will reveal more billabongs which are also safe for swimming.

The best time to come is on an incoming spring tide, so you've got enough time to get in, spend some time here and get out before the water drops again.

MONTGOMERY REEF (YOWJAB) 91/100 □

This amazing reef rises from the sea as the tide recedes.

As each enormous Kimberley tide retreats, Montgomery Reef appears to rise out of the sea, shedding water in spectacular cascades and countless waterfalls. Marine creatures race over the edge of the rapidly drying reef to the safety of the sea, creating stunning scenes unequalled anywhere in the country. Needless to say, the reef is most dramatic during a spring or king tide. It was given its western name by explorer Phillip Parker King, who named it after ship's surgeon Andrew Montgomery in 1818. In the Dambeemangarddee language, this area is known as Yowjab.

At over 300km^2, this is Australia's largest inshore reef, found 20km off the central Kimberley Coast within the 7,000km^2

Lalang-garram / Camden Sound Marine Park. To the Dambeemangarddee, Lalang-garram means "the saltwater as a spiritual place as well as a place of natural abundance" and it hosts the world's biggest humpback whale population. If you arrive between July and October, you'll be treated to incredible encounters with these gentle giants as they feed and breed.

Apart from its great variety of vibrant, coloured coral, the reef is also home to Australian snubfin and Indo-Pacific humpback dolphins, dugongs and threatened marine turtles. Even estuarine crocodiles have been spotted sunbaking on the reef. The late Malcolm Douglas also featured Montgomery Reef in a few of his adventure documentaries. I recommend *Beyond the Kimberley Coast*, in which he travelled to the reef with Indigenous locals and camped on the islands.

On Montgomery Reef's eastern edge, the High Cliffy Islands were home to the Yawijibaya people for over 7,000 years, who eked out a living hunting marine life on the reef. It's said many were over 2m tall, and they navigated the reef on mangrove rafts, using the massive tidal flows to their advantage. Then, mysteriously, soon after a film crew visited in 1929, the tribe of roughly 300 people vanished, and no one knows why.

01 At over 300km^2, Montgomery is Australia's largest inshore reef

02 Turtles and other marine animals race over the edge of the reef as the tide receeds

PRINCE REGENT RIVER 92/100 ☐

Waterfalls and wildlife aplenty

Named after King George IV before he became king, Prince Regent River runs almost dead straight as it follows a fault line to the Saint George Basin. It's a wildlife haven, with more than half the bird and mammal species found in the Kimberley spotted in the Prince Regent National Park. A favourite destination for commercial cruise liners and private yachties, the river has incredible anchorages and swimming spots (well above the saltwater).

One such anchorage is King Cascade (Mambulbada). After idling through a gap in the mangroves, this cascade bedazzles as the view opens before your eyes. Its terraced rock face creates a tapestry of white water, cascading past rock figs and ferns from a freshwater billabong high above. Such is its grandeur that explorer Phillip Parker King gave the waterfall his own name after visiting back in 1820 aboard the Mermaid.

The best time to visit is from March to May, at the tail end of the wet season when the waterfall gushes from recent rainfalls. At the base of the cascade, your boat can nose right up under the falls to give you a freshwater shower. However, due to the presence of salties, swimming below the cascade is entirely off-limits. In 1987, American woman Ginger Meadows was stalked and killed by a saltwater crocodile after she panicked and attempted to swim to a nearby boat from the bottom ledge of the falls. For a safe-from-salties swim, climb up to the pool above the waterfall. Be very careful when scaling up the rocks, as they can be slippery and dangerous.

If you're in the area straight after a good dump of rain, you may be lucky enough to see the Prince Regent Amphitheatre pumping. Tidal movements make this a tricky spot to reach, but if you push on 8km beyond the King Cascade, navigating upstream through mangroves and a narrow gorge, you'll finally set eyes upon glorious Cathedral Falls. Cascading into the cavernous Prince Regent Amphitheatre, this stunning fall drops 75m. The fun part is when your boat cruises right up to the falls for a tropical dunking!

Backtracking towards the mouth of the Prince Regent, you'll find Camp Creek (Banjaddoo). At Camp Creek, you can follow the freshwater upstream through rapids and billabongs and discover two deep, blue swimming holes with gorgeous, paperbark-fringed waterfalls. Swim straight up to the waterfall, take a daring leap off the jump rock (always check the depth first), or just lay back and relax. Of all the great spots to swim in the Kimberley, Camp Creek is one of the prettiest and swimmable year-round.

02

01 Prince Regent Amphitheatre

02 Climb to the top of the King Cascade for a swim above the falls

03 Prince Regent Amphitheatre only runs straight after Wet Season rainfall

03

HUNTER RIVER 93/100 ☐

Scenic anchorages, great fishing and crocs galore

In the northeast corner of the stunning Prince Frederick Harbour, the Hunter River's grandeur can be felt as soon as you reach its river mouth. Here, Kampamantiya, a 200m-high sandstone escarpment, towers overhead. The river is home to one of the largest populations of estuarine crocodiles in the Kimberley, which hints that the barramundi must be in good supply here.

This scenic river winds upstream for 30km, replenished by two 90m-high seasonal waterfalls, the Hunter and Donkins. Bordered by sandstone cliffs, rainforests and mangroves, the river is a spiritual place for the traditional Wunambal Gaambera people, and with anchorages aplenty, it's a favourite for cruising vessels too.

The fishing and crabbing are epic anytime you're here, but the best times are during the run-off, between March and May.

Within the Hunter River, you'll find Porosus Creek, named by the explorer Phillip Parker King. In 1820, when he searched for fresh water, so many salties – Crocodylus porosus – stalked his boat, he named the creek for them. The crocs still thrive today, and a trip up Porosus Creek has lost none of its thrill. Huge salties slide into the water, line the banks and swim, unseen, beneath the boats. There are Brahminy kites and great billed herons, and on the right tide, this is a great spot to fish for giant threadfin salmon.

Travel to the headwaters of Porous Creek to reach Jackson Falls, a lovely swimming hole that's safely out of reach of salties. It was named by the owner of North Star Cruises after his son, Jackson.

THE DC3 AT VANSITTART BAY (BANJAL)

The intact wreck of a DC3 that crashed in 1942

For visitors to remote Vansittart Bay, the wreck of this USAAF Air Transport Command C-53 Skytrooper on the eastern shore of Vansittart is a fascinating (and unexpected) sight. This DC3 crashed en route from Perth to Broome back in February 1942 after the disoriented pilot made an emergency landing in bad weather on a salt pan on the western side of Mungalalu Truscott Airbase.

To the pilot's credit, all crew and passengers survived, and their Kimberley adventure continued when, days later, they were rescued by a passing QANTAS flying boat.

Despite years of battering by storms and fires, the wreck is still in good condition and is a unique stopover on cruise itineraries. Keep an eye out in the surrounding woodland for native wattle trees and colourful rainbow bee-eaters (their whirring whistle is distinct and easy to hear, if you tune in).

Vansittart Bay is located in Wunambal Gaambera Country, known to them as Banjal. With a sandy beach and sandstone outcrops, it has traditionally been used as a fishing place, and middens from shellfish can be found. Private visitors must purchase an Uunguu Visitor Pass, but tour operators will arrange this if you join them. Find out more about visitor passes on page 25.

MERMAID BOAB 95/100 ☐

An old boab tree graffitied by early explorers

While charting the Kimberley coastline in September 1820, Phillip Parker King pulled into a beach, now known as Careening Bay, to repair rotten timber in the hull of his 76-tonne cutter, the *HMC Mermaid*.

The bay provided good shelter and access to fresh water, and Parker King was able to use metal salvaged from a nearby shipwreck to conduct repairs. While there, the ship's carpenter carved "HMC Mermaid" into a nearby boab tree, and almost two centuries later, it remains clearly visible.

The twin-trunked boab is now about 12m in circumference and it is National Heritage-listed. This is the only known monument from King's voyage along the Kimberley coast. With the site receiving more and more visitors, in 2011, Uunguu rangers helped construct a boardwalk to safeguard the tree's root system from tourists' trampling feet.

The Wunambal Gaambera peoples have a historical connection with this place, as their ancestors once lived at the southern part of Careening Bay, where there is a grove of cycads. They ask that you do not remove shells from the beach.

FARAWAY BAY 96/100 ☐

A remote camp pioneered by Bruce and Robyn Ellison in 1986

Have you ever been this far away? Even if you have, Faraway Bay, 280km northwest of Kununurra, is guaranteed to be unlike anywhere you've been before.

Pioneered by my friends Bruce and Robyn Ellison back in 1986 (imagine being up here during that time), Faraway's bush camp consists of eight simple but comfortable cabins with ensuites (which I helped rebuild after Cyclone Ingrid in 2005). All are positioned along the cliffs with commanding views over the Timor Sea. You can float in the small freshwater plunge pool, enjoy canapés at sunset and fill long days exploring on the water. In my opinion, the real charm is the reality of being so remote, although the evenings spent around the dining table, yarning with other guests, is pretty special.

The number one thing to do here is to visit the magnificent King George River and falls, which are a half-day boat trip away. Even though the falls turn to a trickle after the wet season, cruising through the gorge is always mind-blowing! At the nearby Lost City, you'll see galleries of ancient Gwion Gwion rock art (read more about this art on page 39). Plus, the fishing in this corner of the Kimberley is fantastic, and the stargazing is next level because there is zero light pollution. There is also zero road access, so you'll need to charter a flight from Kununurra (one hour) or Darwin (90 minutes). You can arrange this when booking through farawaybay.com.au.

KING GEORGE FALLS (OOMARRI) 97/100 ☐

Nothing beats a new day breaking in the ancient King George River

The sound of bird calls echoing through the gorge, schools of fish ripping across the surface and the roar of mighty waterfalls, are sights and sounds that will stay with you forever.

To the Balanggarra people, this is Oomarri: home to breathtaking gorges and WA's tallest duo of waterfalls that drop 100m over the edge of the escarpment. To the Balanggarra people, the sacred twin falls of Oomarri represent the male and female Wunkurr (rainbow serpents). As such, they ask visitors not to climb to the top of the falls without prior permission.

This area is widely known as one of the most pristine, untouched wilderness areas on the planet. No matter what time of year you visit, you'll be spellbound by this magnificent gorge. At the tail end of the Wet

01 As the Dry Season progresses, the waterfalls turn to a trickle

02 Straight after a fresh dump of rain at the end of the Wet Season (March)

Season (March), rain swells the King George River, turning it into a raging torrent that tumbles over the sandstone cliffs and into the tidal waters below. When King George Falls dries to a trickle during the Dry Season, boats can anchor close, sometimes directly beneath (what remains of) the falls. No matter what time of year you visit, the gorge is incredible.

Scenic flights will get you here year-round, or you can join a cruise during the Dry Season.

BERKELEY RIVER LODGE 98/100 ☐

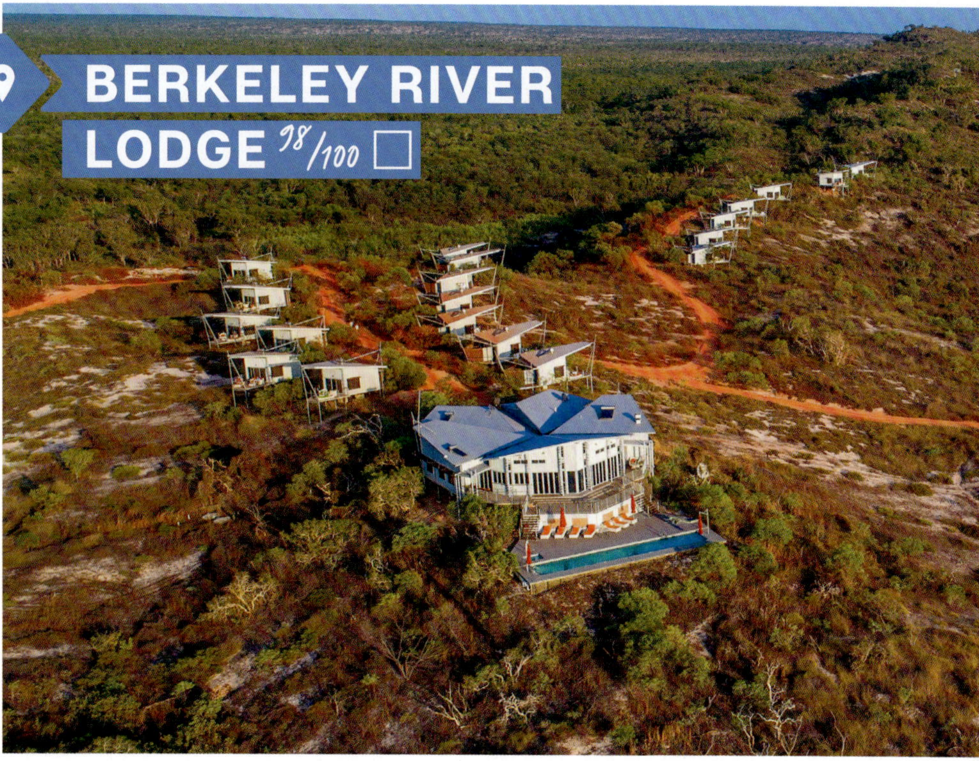

Gorges, fishing and a 5-star, oceanfront lodge

So far from civilisation, there are very few developments along the Kimberley coastline. This is part of what makes the Berkeley River Lodge such a stunning escape. That and the spectacular 135km-long Berkeley River, which winds through the Oombulgurri Indigenous Reserve before emptying into the Joseph Bonaparte Gulf. This is the country of the Balanggarra people, and it is ruggedly stunning and abundant in fish and wildlife.

Stays at the luxurious river lodge offer unparalleled access to a remote river wilderness: rugged gorges, waterfalls and soaring sandstone cliffs. Waterfalls gush straight after rain, usually from March to May. And barra fishing is also best at this time of year. To experience it all, the Lodge offers small-group scenic river cruises, safari-inspired beach adventures, creek nature walks, fishing expeditions and scenic helicopter flights. Plus, the sunsets here are glorious.

Private villas at Berkeley's exclusive resort overlook the sea, and the outdoor bathrooms are spot-on. The swimming pool showcases expansive vistas of the river mouth and coastal escarpments. Access is only via light aircraft from Kununurra or Darwin, landing at Berkeley's private airstrip, proving how remote it really is. The lodge caters for a maximum of 40 people at a time. Once you're there, everything is included, except for chopper flights (I recommend the heli-fishing tour, whether you're a keen angler or even an amateur). See more at berkeleyriverlodge.com.au.

01 The lodge has glorious vistas out over the Timor Sea

02 The 135km Berkeley River has scenic vistas and great fishing

THE ROWLEY SHOALS 99/100 ☐

World-class diving and snorkelling, far off the coast

If you're looking for a good dose of vitamin sea, an expedition to the Rowley Shoals might be just what the doctor ordered! Located 160 nautical miles (296km) west of Broome on the edge of one of the widest continental shelves in the world, Rowley Shoals Marine Park is a snorkellers' paradise.

Here, crystal clear waters and tropical temperatures make for exceptional snorkelling and diving, quite unlike anywhere else in Australia. The sea temperatures – 23 to 30°C – are fantastic. There's no need for a wetsuit here! There's also excellent fishing in certain areas of the shoals with big, blue-water pelagics such as sailfish, black marlin, wahoo and yellowfin tuna commonly targeted, tagged and released.

What lures snorkellers so far off the coast are three huge coral atolls that rise 400m from the seabed, each covering vast distances of 80 to 90km^2 and harbouring shallow, coral-filled lagoons. At low tide, turquoise ponds trapped inside the reef walls resemble big, glassy swimming pools in the middle of the ocean. The ebb and flow of the tides have greatly encouraged

the marine environment here, with oversized corals prospering in the nutrient-rich waters. The time to come is September to November when local doldrums create light winds and glassy seas. Just a small handful of commercial operators come out here – check out therowleyshoals.com.au.

When the reef disappears with the high tide, the sandy Clerke and Imperieuse Islands are the only dry land for miles and idyllic spots to soak up the sunshine and pretend the rest of the world doesn't exist. If you're a water baby, this is the place for you. Prepare for endless blue scenes by day and stars reflected in glassy seas by night.

01 Relaxing on the sand cay that is Bedwell Island

02 There's no need for a wetsuit when the water temperatures are 23 to 30°C

03 BYO stand-up paddleboard

SCOTT REEF 100/100 ☐

The search ends here

I thought it would be cool to end this book with a new addition, and a reef I share a name with. As one of only a few offshore reefs in the northwest, Scott Reef has always been a spot that only a handful of people know about. Until now, I haven't been able to get my hands on a photo, but thanks to my old schoolmate Tao Hoogland (who provided these ones), I've finally included it in this list.

Scott Reef has all the right ingredients to be seen in one of Rip Curl's 'The Search' billboards – amazing, empty, fun waves barrelling off a reef somewhere near the equator. While it's not on the mainland Kimberley, access is from Broome (280 nautical miles northwest of Broome – an overnight steam), with only a few cruise boats offering trips out here. The catamaran *Karma IV* (owned by my Broome mate Chaz Kennedy) has been coming out here for years, and Tao charters the boat for a couple of trips a year for keen surfers and spearfishermen.

Like the Rowley Shoals, this spot sits on the continental shelf, and the coral reefs are abundant with all kinds of marine life. There are more than 300 species of reef-building corals, a whopping 720 fish species, 400 mollusc species and about 118 crustacean species. With two separate reef platforms (North Reef and South Reef) rising steeply from the continental shelf, snorkelling and freediving are out of this world. The area is also visited by humpback whales and whale sharks in season, and two kinds of marine turtles nest here.

But the cherry on top of it all is the surf; if you're lucky enough to get it when it's doing its thing, you'll have world-class waves all to yourself.

The game fishing here is also amazing, with species such as yellowfin and dog tooth tuna, sailfish and wahoo. Check out solunaretreat.org for Tao's trips or for info about the boat visit karma4.com.au. For a bigger boat, Seae Star Boat Charters also runs charters. seaestarboatcharters.com.au.

Exploring Eden Media

100 Things to See In The Kimberley: 2nd Editon was first published in 2023 by Exploring Eden Media

ISBN: 978-0-6455226-4-8

All enquiries should be made to:

Exploring Eden Media Pty Ltd
250 Princes Highway, Bulli, NSW, 2516
publications@exploringedenmedia.com

NATIONAL LIBRARY OF AUSTRALIA

A catalogue record for this book is available from the National Library of Australia

Author: Scotty Connell
Publisher: Melissa Thimios
Editor: Brendan Batty
Design: Matthew Ware, OBJKTIVE

Printed in China by C & C Offset Printing

FSC® MIX Paper | Supporting responsible forestry FSC® C008047 www.fsc.org

The paper used in this book has been sourced from sustainable forests certified by Forest Stewardship Council® as part of our commitment to environmental responsibility. Find out more at fsc.org.

Disclaimer

Some of the activities mentioned in this book are dangerous and many of the regions are wild and remote. Consider your own safety and that of your companions when undertaking travel or participating in activities referenced within, which you undertake at your own risk. The maps contained within are soley for illustration purposes and should not be relied upon for navigation.

PICTURE CREDITS

Chris Magnay, @magnay; cover, **149, 150**
Salty Wings, @saltywings; inside front cover, **14, 16, 24, 26, 29, 30, 35, 45, 47, 78, 80, 81, 136, 137, 184, 195, 218, 219, 224**
Charlotte and James Maddock, @cjmaddock; **10, 41, 46, 58, 60, 96, 167, 177**
Tom DeSouza, @storiesfromthescenicroute; **12**
Sean Scott, @seanscottphotography; **18, 110, 223**
Cygnet Bay Pearl Farm, @cygnetbaypearlfarm; **28, 42, 65, 75, 76, 77**
Tourism Australia/Brinkley Davies; **37, 144, 145, 157, 161**
Warmun Art Centre, @warmunart; **37**
Tao Hoogland, @taos_oceanadventure **45, 59, 220, 221**
Tourism Australia/Jarrad Seng; **48, 50, 57, 66, 189**
Tourism Australia/Jampal Dawa; **45, 47, 49**
iStock; **52, 108, 146**
Tourism Australia/Matsos Brewery; **56**
Martin Long, Ginreab Thai; **56**
The Mango Place, @themangoplace; **56**
Tourism Australia/Matt Deakin; **61, 71, 182**
Elise Cook, @elise cook; **62, 106, 113, 132, 157**
Lisa Watkins, @wherethewatos; **65, 69**
Kat Doyle, @katdoyle.9; **65, 70**
Mariana Dobe, @itsadobeslife; **68**
Charlie Hawkins, @the_travelling_tarts; **69**
Tourism Australia/Warwick Thornton and Brendan Fletcher; **72**
Ardyaloon Hatchery; **73**
Todd Thimios, @toddthimios; **93, 131, 143, 145, 148, 151, 152, 159**
Beth Ironside, @bethybydesign; **94, 155**
Sam Birch, Birchy's Fishing Tours; **102, 103**
Adam Williams; **116**
Shutterstock; **119, 129, 158, 185, 207**
Adam Craze, @crazie01; **126**
Al Mackinnon, @almackinnon; **130, 135**
Adam Mackay, @ordriver; **142, 149**
Brinkley Davies, @brinkleydavies; **147**
Ben Broadwith, @ben_broady; **162**
Tourism Australia/Osprey; **165, 170, 171**
Bungle Bungles Savannah Lodge; **180**
Fitzroy River Lodge; **180**
Mimbi Caves Tours; **180**
Neralie Middleton, facebook.com/willareroadhouse; **188**
Biancavilla Pizza facebook.com/biancavillapizza; **188**
Grace Picot, @shotbygrace; **190, 191**
Larissa, landtosea.com.au; **192**
Tourism Australia/Scott Slawinski; **61, 71, 182, 206, 214**
Wildman Film Productions; **216, 217**
Taminga Connell; **34,** back cover art

From The Publishers

The first edition of *100 Things To See In The Kimberley* was a special project for us, as it was the book that started our little publishing house. Revisiting this book for its second edition has been fun, though a lot has changed since we published the first edition in 2019.

For this second edition, we've adopted the format of our third guide, *100 Things To See on Australia's Coral Coast*, increasing the page count and adding more information on the region's history and heritage, places to eat, sleep, stay and learn. We spent months emailing back and forth with our author, Scotty, who provided new text and images, simultaneously juggling this project with his tourism business operations, his non-profit foundation and his family of eight (including a newborn baby). Typing these words right now, we feel relieved to be completing this intensive project and excited to see people enjoying it!

We want to thank Scotty's family for supporting him during the months that he spent working on this second edition. We also want to thank you, the reader, who is exploring or dreaming about The Kimberley with this guide. Books are pointless without readers, so we hope we've inspired you to enjoy this beautiful part of Australia, to slow down and connect with its people and landscape, and to take in the best bits according to the locals.

Melissa Thimios and Brendan Batty
exploringedenbooks.com
@exploringedenbooks